ONE LIFE. IT'S TIME TO LIVE IT

MY

one life

MY ULTIMATE BUCKET LIST

A catalogue record for this book is available from the British Library.

First published in Great Britain in 2022
by Carpet Bombing Culture.
An imprint of Pro-actif Communications.

Email: books@carpetbombingculture.co.uk

Written by Patrick Potter and Gary Shove

ISBN: 978-1-908211-84-2

www.carpetbombingculture.com

one life

IT'S TIME TO LIVE IT

"
ADVENTURE
IS A MINDSET
- NOT A
BANK BALANCE
"

Welcome to **One Life.** No replays, no extra lives.

No waiting for a more convenient lifetime to arrive.

Life is not elsewhere. Life is not **elsewhen.**

If you don't grab hold of that rudder, this old ship is just going to drift in a torrent of the collected half-assed ideas of random other people with weak imaginations.

You need a treasure map.

Voila, this is it. The Bucket List For Your Soul.

If you knew you had one year to live, what would you do?

This book will help you to answer that question.

With this ultimate bucket list you will:

- Create your own shortlist of things you can actually do in the real world.
- Tick off all the amazing things you've already achieved.
- Get inspired and fired up, blow out the cobwebs and believe in your desires.
- Start audacious conversations with others, make big fat daring plans.
- Learn more about you, what drives you and attracts you.
- Spark real world adventures that will literally change your life.
- Discover small adventures with big impact, available to you right now.
- Make your life story a work of art that will echo through the ages.

Remember: Adventure is a mindset - not a bank balance.

contents

tick it off

DO YOU WANT TO MAKE SOME MEMORIES?

Yes. Yes you do.

Look that child in the eye, the one you used to be, and tell them what you're going to do. Make them proud of you.

Make the universe remember your name.

One Life.

When you're a kid you never doubt for a second that you are the captain of a ship setting sail for adventure. But one day you wake up and realise that you've let go of the helm and if you don't get it back **right now** then when?

A bucket list is both a realisation that nothing lasts forever and a daring and hopeful statement of intent. A bucket list is a way to ensure that your own life story will be worth telling when the final curtain comes down.

But dreaming isn't enough for you anymore.

SO, JUST HOW DO YOU LIVE YOUR BEST LIFE?

Well, first of all, **you have to take your desires seriously.**

This is nothing more complex or mystical than what you already know. You have to figure out what you want, and figure out how to make it happen then...**pull the trigger.**

All of this must be balanced out with your material reality, and the unique set of opportunities and obligations, freedoms and responsibilities, advantages and disadvantages that you face.

This book is about remembering to keep asking yourself those key questions. What do I want? What are my values? How do I want to be seen and remembered?

And it's a book of ideas and inspiration. Try out different ideas for size in the changing rooms of your imagination. Play 'You Choose' with a friend. Pick out your favourites from each section. Remix, change and adapt anything you find.

Finally, it's an actual physical bucket list that you can write in. A rudimentary planning tool for taking that first step from dreaming to living.

This book is where you write and keep your ultimate Bucket List.

HOW DO YOU USE THIS BOOK?

Open your mind. Flip through. Scribble madly.

Sometimes we need reminding of the rich tapestry of possibilities that a ride on the rollercoaster of human life can offer. When you're in need of inspiration, come and browse this buffet of potential experiences, let your mind wander freely and enjoy the resulting fantasies. Play the ideas out in your head. Try to see them, feel them.

It all starts out in your mind's eye.

This book is a menu at a restaurant of potential adventures. It's a starter for conversations with yourself and significant others about your values and desires. It's a napkin for sketching out audacious plans. It's a bottle of fine wine for loosening up your thinking.

It's that one friend who always seems to live life like a viking at a rave, who makes you feel like anything is possible if you just talk your way into it.

Pick out the things you want to do, make them your own and write that dang bucket list.

> **Own the book. Scribble, daub, tear, stick things in and drop it in the bath. Remix and rewrite.**
>
> **Write your own missions from scratch.**

But that's not all - now it's time to actually put those list items into unstoppable motion.

> **Start by making your mouth write cheques
> your ass may not be able to cash.**

When we walk ourselves into a public commitment to something, we'll move mountains not to have to appear inconsistent. We'd rather make it happen than bottle out.

If you've written paragliding on your bucket list, make the initial phone call then tell somebody else that you just made the initial phone call. Now the wheels are in motion. Things build their own momentum.

Always be thinking, what can I do today? What can I do this week, month, year? And if there are obstacles, what steps do I take to get around them? Is there a way to make it cheaper or even free? If I can't do it now, when can I? Can I do the essence of the idea in another place, time or way?

Come back to the book to rewrite and adapt and change the bucket list as you yourself change. Things are always drifting out of reach just as other things are drifting into reach. Time is always giving as it takes away.

Let your Bucket List become a habit of sitting down to have a long conversation with yourself on a regular basis. Review your desires. Celebrate your wins. Share the process with loved ones.

Because **KNOWING YOUR DESIRES** is the only way to **LIVE WITH INTENTION.**

TODAY IS THE FIRST DAY
OF THE REST OF YOUR LIFE

Here it is, take a deep breath, and drink it in. Grab it by the chimichangas, slap it around the falafels and take it out to dinner on a Monday night. This is your life. You own it. You rent it out to other people quite frequently but hey, you gotta make RENT. Who doesn't? So how in the hell are we going to live our BEST LIFE?

We don't know. BUT YOU DO. Probably.

You picked up this book because you want to have more days thriving and fewer days surviving. You are sick of the coasting and want more of the mosting. You don't want to wait. You want to take hold of the goddam steering wheel and turn this ship towards the high seas of a life less ordinary.

Well baby, if you want to be a pirate adventurer you're gonna need a treasure map.

Think about it this way, **you're writing your autobiography backwards.**

Imagine you are sitting in the Sunnyvale Retirement home, in the TV lounge in a rocker by the bay window, gently surrendering yourself to fabulous decay, in no way regretting the tattoos. In between naps, you are dictating your exploits to a young version of yourself, who sits enraptured at the scandalous tales of 'derring do'. **Je ne regrette rien.**

What stories are you telling? - This is your bucket list.

So what is going to be in those stories? Vegas? The Great Wall of China? The Maldives?

Other Bucket List books are basically just long lists of bougie travel destinations - but not this one. Sure, travel is awesome, but these days the tick list traveller seems just a little out of step with the times. And the times, they are a' changin...

In the olden days, before the pandemics and the wildfires, the killer heatwaves, the sinking nations, a Bucket List was a different kind of a beast.

When we lived in the eternal party of the Fossil Fuel Age, a Bucket List was often simply a list of very expensive world travel destinations.

Now, as it seems ever more likely that the **low cost flight** will become a thing of legend whispered about by the elders, conspicuous consumption doesn't seem quite as appealing as it once did.

Conspicuous consumption has gone as far as it can go, when people pay thousands of dollars to stage photos that make it look like they're spending millions. It's all getting a little bit Great Gatsby, and we all know what happened after the Roaring Twenties reached their dizzying conclusions last time around.

So what is a Bucket List in the age of the Climate Crisis?

Well, we don't know any better than you do. But we've had a go.

And this is our attempt at a starting point for **your journey of answering that question for yourself.** We defeated the blank page on your behalf to give you a wall of words to bounce off. (And we collected together as many mixed metaphors as we could stomach.)

So is anyone going to attempt to answer the title question? I suppose we must.

So, how do you use this book?

First, understand that we have attempted to define three categories of LIST ITEMS for your BUCKET LIST.

Adventures are things that you go out to do, braving the unknown, taking risks and learning stuff about yourself in the process. A typical adventure might be visiting somewhere for the first time or heading off to do a pilgrimage.

Experiences are things that you just go to soak up and be a part of, often events. A typical experience would be going to a famous festival or trying a new type of food.

Growth contains items for your list that will generally take a bit more time and effort to make happen. Typical achievements would be learning a language or starting a podcast.

Use these sections to populate your Bucket List. Use them to inspire you to write your own items from scratch, or even maybe your own categories. Flick through, read a bit, daydream a lot. Remember how to believe in the reality of your desires.

The final two sections of each of the three categories encourage you to do exactly that, write your BUCKET LIST into the very pages of this book, creating the special and ancient magic of focussed intention that writing by hand is especially good for.

We hope you find some inspiration here, and of course it's even more fun if you use it with friends, partners, family and lovers. If you hate it tell us, if you love it, tell everyone.

Even now the world around is seething with possibilities. We are trapped in cages of our own making. Our perspective hides from us many things that only a small shift in that perspective might reveal. What if I looked at myself through the eyes of someone else for a moment? What thought experiments could I do right now to break open the way I look at today, this week, this year?

Because there are eight billion of us, and your situation is never totally unique, and there is always someone out there who has faced exactly the same conditions that you face right now and then gone and done something you would never have dreamed was possible.

And when you boil it down, what is this drive towards adventure except a hunger for renewal, renewal that comes through the breaking open of the crust of the old world view, to clear a space in the rubble of your psyche to build a new version of you.

THE FUTURE
STARTS
RIGHT NOW...

RIGHT HERE, RIGHT NOW

The person to call

The place to go

The question to ask

The journey to plan

The goal to set

The commitment to make

The promise to make

The thing to forget

The plans to make

"
shooting
for moons
"

Welcome to the rest of your life. Buckle up, keep your hands inside the ride and try not to scare the children. We're about to raise our sights, our hopes and our expectations. We're about to broadcast our desires to the four corners of the known universe. When you write your dreams down, it's like black magic, turning fantasies into plans, aspirations into steps.

It's time to get busy on the bucket list.

How would you live if you knew your life was a brief and fleeting moment in the torrential river of history? Oh wait.

Don't panic.

Let's open up a space for your imagination.

Number one: Many more things are possible than you realise, even without throwing in your day job and shirking your responsibilities to walk barefoot in the mountains writing haiku.

Number two: Taking your desires seriously will enrich your life and the lives of others. Making experiences, adventures and growth a priority will raise the consciousness of the entire species.

Number three: Making a bucket list is just plain fun and you get to enjoy the process, even if the meteor hits tomorrow and you never get to tick off a single damn thing.

Welcome to One Life, where you, hurtling through the void clinging to a giant rock at 67, 000 miles per hour, an absurd being who has the audacity to feel something called 'bored' and has decided to somehow LIVE A BIGGER LIFE.

Very well,
let us begin...

How does one 'Bucket List'
like an absolute boss?

An excellent question.

Do that thing that you never do anymore. Give
yourself some time to think. Give yourself
permission to daydream, to explore yourself, to
imagine a world in which everything is possible.

Step 1: Hold your calls, switch off your phone,
stop rushing around, breathe, switch off the
boxset and quit the scrolling. Get out the wine,
or the chocolate or whatever it is that makes
you feel indulgent. Slow. the. frack. down.

Step 2: Get into a playful, curious mindset. Silence all those grown up voices in your head. No limits. No analysis. No judgement.

Step 3: Explore the book, asking yourself only - what am I attracted to most strongly? Which of these ideas sparks fire in my belly? Which of these ideas makes me smile? What would I do if there was no force on earth that could stop me? What would I do in a world without limits?

Step 4: Now ask yourself...'Can I adapt, change or merge any of these ideas to make them even more exciting to me?'

TL;DR - Allow yourself to have your wildest and most free dreams and desires then step back and use your genius to adapt items on your list to make them really achievable within a specific time frame.

"Take it from dream list to task list.

Now you are a bucket list boss!"

adventures

A LIFE LESS ORDINARY

Next time you find yourself out running, cycling or walking, take a random turn down a road you've never been down.

Suddenly your whole perception shifts.

You amplify the amount of sensory information that you actually pay attention to.

...You drink it in.

Your brain is writing new maps, parsing and storing all the new data. You might get lost. You might end up going way off course and coming back some random way. You may end up being late for the rest of the day. Adventures always carry a price.

You've traded off controlled risk, a dose of uncertainty for a few minutes of feeling more present, more alive. It's bizarrely satisfying for a very modest gesture of spontaneity.

This is the baseline definition of an adventure. It is the **'hero's journey'** in miniature.

Adventures are often right under our noses. Adventures are very much a shift of perspective, a way of seeing. Looking for small adventures on a daily basis is awesome.

But every now and then, you'll want to go large on that.

Big adventures are just plain bigger, and the risks and the payoffs are bigger too.

Some adventures are beyond the scope of this book: Grow up - Make a decent living in difficult times - Fall in love - Make babies - Raise them up full grown.

Massive great terrifying lifelong adventures those are. But you, you reckless and beautiful savage, you are not satisfied. You want to play the game of life on hard mode.

In-between those epic life-adventure sagas, you want even more adventures. You want to cram every nook and cranny of your lived experience with adventures big and small.

You want to live a life the gods will remember.

So, we've done our damnedest to gather together a smorgasbord of delectable adventures for your perusal here. Raise your drinking horn you bloody legend!

Here's to a life less ordinary!

MY ADVENTURES

One minute you're happy eating seed cake and smoking your pipe in the garden, the next minute an old man with a big beard and a funny hat persuades you to go and steal a massive diamond from a dragon. It doesn't always happen like that, but pretty much.

Adventures. When we're kids it's literally all we want from life. And that's OK because we can play at being adventurers and are generally quite satisfied with that. But when we get bigger, something within pulls at us to do something a little more...real.

Then life takes over, and we find ourselves drowning in commitments and responsibilities and financial limitations.

Do we have to give up on these childish dreams of adventure?

Perhaps not.

Some are born to adventure, some achieve adventure and some have adventure thrust upon them.

Which will you be?

WHAT IS AN ADVENTURE?

Our greatest strength is our greatest weakness, our adaptability. We can get used to anything. And once we get used to something, we do it on autopilot. When we coast through the days and weeks and months and years on autopilot, time whistles past our ears at a terrifying velocity.

It takes the shock of the new to wake us up. Some kind of ferocious one-handed slap to make us use every little part of our attention on what is actually happening right now. And then we grow, because we have to suddenly design a bigger version of ourselves to include the new experience.

Adventure must then include some element of risk, some kind of discomfort, and some experience of the as yet unknown. It must involve crossing a barrier as yet uncrossed.

An adventure can be small or epic. But it has to change you.

If you're not late for dinner, it doesn't count.

GREAT ESCAPES

The world really is out there. It really is.

And you can go and be in it. It's deceptively easy.

Mostly we don't because it's always so much easier not to.
The longing to go beyond the boundaries of our daily reality,
is ancient. We travel because we must cross fertilise our
cultures, our ideas.

Bucket *Done it*

Raft the Grand Canyon, Colorado, USA

Walk The Via Dolorosa (Way of Sorrow)
following the Stations of the Cross in Jerusalem

Ride in a classic car in Havana, Cuba

Take a black cab in London

Take a ride in a Gondola in Venice, Italy

Ride the Great Smokey Mountain Railroad, North
Carolina, USA

Drive Route 66, Chicago to Los Angeles, USA

Ride on an Airboat through the Everglades

Cycle along the canals of Amsterdam, Netherlands

Bucket *Done it*

- Set foot on Antarctica

- Climb Kilimanjaro, Tanzania

- Get lost in New York City, USA

- Hike the Appalachian Trail, West Virginia, USA

- Walk on the Giants Causeway, Northern Ireland

- Hike in the Canadian Rockies, Canada

- Wander round Pere-Lachaise Cemetery, Paris, France

- Marvel at the Aurora Borealis (Northern Lights) Sweden, Finland, Norway, Russia, Canada, Alaska, Southern Greenland

- Visit the vineyards of Tuscany

- Watch the Bolshoi Ballet, Moscow, Russia

- See the Berlin Wall, Berlin, Germany

- Ride a bike round Central Park, New York, USA

- Visit Anne Frank's House, Amsterdam, Netherlands

Bucket Done it

○ ○   Celebrate Hogmanay in Edinburgh Scotland

○ ○   Take part in a debate at Speakers' Corner,
Hyde Park, London, England

○ ○   Visit Dracula's Castle, Bran Castle, Bran, Romania

○ ○   Ride in a yellow cab in New York

○ ○   Go to the Cannes Film Festival, Cannes, France

○ ○   Have a Turkish bath in Istanbul, Turkey

○ ○   Ride the rollercoaster at Coney Island, New York,
USA.

○ ○   Stay at Banksy's Walled Off Hotel in Bethlehem,
Palestine

○ ○   Marvel at the Ruins of Petra, Jordan

○ ○   Look for aliens at Area 51, Nevada, USA

○ ○   Explore underground through The Catacombs of
Paris, France

○ ○   Visit St Mark's Basilica, Venice, Italy

○ ○   Cross the Golden Gate Bridge, San Francisco,
California, USA

Bucket *Done it*

○ ○ See The Parthenon, Athens, Greece

○ ○ Celebrate Christmas in Bethlehem, Palestine

○ ○ Walk along The Great Wall of China, Northern China

○ ○ Watch Flamenco Dancing in Andalucia, Spain

○ ○ Listen to Fado Music in Lisbon, Portugal

○ ○ See The Forbidden City, Beijing, China

○ ○ Party All Night on the Beach at a Full Moon Rave on Ko Pha-ngan, Thailand

○ ○ Walk the Hollywood Walk of Fame, Los Angeles, California, USA

○ ○ Watch a space rocket launch, Kennedy Space Centre, Florida, USA

○ ○ Ride a street car in San Francisco, California, USA

○ ○ Take a trip to see the Nazca Lines in Peru

○ ○ Visit the Gaudi's The Basílica de la Sagrada Família in Barcelona, Spain

Bucket   Done it

○ ○   See Michelangelo's 'The Creation of Adam',
       The Vatican, Vatican City, Rome, Italy

○ ○   Go clubbing at a super club in Ibiza,
       Balearic Islands, Spain

○ ○   See the Niagara Falls, Canada/USA

○ ○   Visit all 50 states in the USA

○ ○   View the beautiful colours during fall in Maine, USA

○ ○   Make a pilgrimage to The Church of the Nativity,
       Bethlehem, Palestine

○ ○   Visit The Western Wall, Jerusalem, Israel

○ ○   Meditate at a Thai Monastery in Bangkok, Thailand

○ ○   Marvel at the giant Redwoods of Sequoia National
       Park, California, USA

○ ○   Contemplate the wonder of Stonehenge, Salisbury
       Plain, Wiltshire, England

○ ○   Browse a Christmas Market in Germany

○ ○   See the fairytale Castle at Neuschwantein,
       Schwangau, Germany

Bucket *Done it*

○ ○ Explore the Mayan ruins at Chichen Itza, Mexico

○ ○ Spot the big five wild animals: Lion, Leopard, Rhino, Elephant and African Buffalo on an African safari

○ ○ Listen the chimes of Big Ben, London, England

○ ○ Make a wish by throwing a coin in the Trevi Fountain, Rome, Italy

○ ○ Go skiing in the Alps

○ ○ Watch a traditional regional folk dance in Greece

○ ○ Watch a belly dance show in Istanbul, Turkey

○ ○ Bathe in the Széchenyi Thermal Spa Baths in Budapest, Hungary

○ ○ Journey to the sacred Batu Caves, Gombak, Selangor, Malaysia

○ ○ Take a selfie in front of the Hollywood sign, Los Angeles, California, USA

○ ○ Contemplate history on a guided tour around Auschwitz Concentration Camp, Oswiecim, Poland

Bucket   *Done it*

- ⚪ ⚪ Watch The Changing of the Guard in front of Buckingham Palace, London, England

- ⚪ ⚪ Marvel at the floating markets of Bangkok, Thailand

- ⚪ ⚪ Listen to the street musicians of New Orleans, Louisiana, USA

- ⚪ ⚪ Enjoy gelato in Rome, Italy

- ⚪ ⚪ Enjoy Key Lime Pie in Key West, Florida, USA

- ⚪ ⚪ Make a declaration of love at the Taj Mahal, India

- ⚪ ⚪ Take a long train journey across multiple countries

- ⚪ ⚪ Take a trip with my parents

- ⚪ ⚪ Take a trip with my children

- ⚪ ⚪ Explore the Mayan ruins of Tikal, Guatemala

- ⚪ ⚪ Drive the length of Highway 1, California, USA

- ⚪ ⚪ Cruise down the Nile on a traditional Dahabiya, Egypt

- ⚪ ⚪ Throw a dart at a map and just go

EMPIRES & CIVILISATIONS

If you want to understand our current reality, play history backwards. Can you imagine standing where Julius Ceasar was murdered, walking streets that the Pharaohs walked, standing in a Roman laundry or a Sultan's harem? There are places so drenched in history it sends shivers down your spine. Stand where the guillotines stood in the French revolution, walk around the Aztec remains of Teotihuacán in Mexico. The list is endless.

Bucket *Done it*

- Roman Empire circa 550 BC–465 AD – Rome, Italy
- Mayan circa 2600 BC–900 AD – Mexico/Guatemala/Belize/El Salvador/Honduras
- Incan circa 1438 AD–1532 AD – Eduador/Peru/Chile
- Aztec circa 1325 AD–1521 AD - Mexico
- Ancient Egyptian circa 3150 BC–30 B.C. - Egypt
- Byzantine Empire circa 330 AD-1453 AD - Turkey
- Mesopotamia circa 3500 BC–500 BC - Iraq, Syria, and Turkey
- Ancient Greek – circa 2700 BC–479 BC - Greece
- Persia circa 550 BC–331 BC - Iran
- Chinese Civilisation circa 1600 BC–1046 BC - China
- Indus Valley circa 3300 BC–1900 BC - Northeast Afghanistan to Pakistan and Northwest India
- Australian Aboriginals circa 50,000 BC - Present Day Australia

"

wanderlust

"

Humans need to explore.

To stand at the water's edge and stare
longingly at the horizon is as old as humanity.

We are a species that is always wondering just
what the heck is over the next hill.

And now, as a result, we have colonised every
biome on the globe.

But we still need to travel. Because we never
really know our home until we've been away.

We leave so that we can return.

Our tragedy is that we can get used to anything. We take things for granted. People who live in Paris never go up the Eiffel Tower.

But there are ways you can trick yourself into seeing what is really there, into seeing the world around you as if it were some new exotic land. Making art is one way. Travel is another.

Going away is important, even if the world gets a little more careful. In the near future it seems likely that we may go away less often, or less far. So it's good to know that sometimes just walking to the next town can give you the same experience of renewed vision, fresh ideas and inspiration as a trip to the Great Wall of China or the Hanging Gardens of Babylon.

And when you do get the chance to go on a truly epic trip, you'll appreciate it all the more. It's too easy to miss the real deep fascinations of a historic site when you experience it all from the other side of your smartphone camera.

"
Don't waste your adventures on feeding the algorithms.
"

100 PLACES TO GO

Once the grand tour was the education of the young aristocrat. Now the world has changed again. Seek quality not quantity. A place is never simply a place. How you arrive in it is everything.

- The Doge's Palace and St Marks Square, Venice, Italy

- La Tomatina Festival, Bunol, Spain

- Empire State Building, New York, USA

- St Mark's Basilica, Venice, Italy

- Eiffel Tower, Paris, France

- Universal Studios, Los Angeles, California USA

- Ayers Rock, Australia

- The Pyramids of Giza and Great Sphinx, Cairo, Egypt

- The Colosseum, Rome, Italy

- Taj Mahal, Agra, India

- Chernobyl, Pripyat, Ukraine

- The Church of the Holy Sepulchre, Jerusalem

- The Sagrada Familia, Barcelona, Spain

	Bucket	Done it

Gyeongbokgung Palace, Seoul, South Korea

The Pantheon, Rome, Italy

Great Barrier Reef, Queensland, Australia

Christ the Redeemer, Rio de Janeiro, Brazil

Table Mountain, Cape Town, South Africa

Blue Mosque, Istanbul, Turkey

Notre Dame Cathedral, Paris, France

Disney World, Florida, USA

Szechenyi Baths, Budapest, Hungary

The Sistine Chapel, Vatican City, Rome, Italy

Berlin Wall, Berlin, Germany

Rialto Bridge, Venice, Italy

Hagia Sophia, Istanbul, Turkey

Niagara Falls, Canada/USA

Edinburgh Castle, Edinburgh, Scotland

Las Vegas Strip, Las Vegas, USA

The Acropolis, Athens, Greece

Bucket Done it

○ ○ Buckingham Palace, London, England

○ ○ The Statue of Liberty, New York, USA

○ ○ The Forum, Rome, Italy

○ ○ The Forbidden City, Beijing, China

○ ○ Roman Ruins of Pompeii, Italy

○ ○ The Medina, Marrakesh, Morocco

○ ○ The Great Pyramid of Giza, Egypt

○ ○ The Terracotta Army, Lintong District, Xi'an, Shaanxi, China

○ ○ The Dead Sea, Jordan

○ ○ The Sahara Desert, North Africa

○ ○ Milan Cathedral, Milan, Italy

○ ○ Bagan's Temples, Myanmar

○ ○ Petra, Jordan

○ ○ The Summer Palace, Beijing, China

○ ○ The WWII Beaches of Normandy, France

○ ○ The Giant's Causeway, Northern Ireland

○ ○ The Canals of Amsterdam, Netherlands

Bucket *Done it*

◐ ◑ Times Square, New York, USA

◐ ◑ Leaning Tower of Pisa, Italy

◐ ◑ Santorini, Cyclades Islands, Greece

◐ ◑ The Wailing Wall and Temple Mount, Jerusalem, Israel

◐ ◑ Saint Basil's Cathedral, Red Square, Moscow, Russia

◐ ◑ The Golden Temple, Armritsar, Punjab, India

◐ ◑ Prague Castle, Prague, Czech Republic

◐ ◑ The Parthenon, Athens, Greece

◐ ◑ Burj Khalifa, Dubai, UAE

◐ ◑ Neuschwanstein Castle, Hohenschwangau, Southwest Bavaria, Germany

◐ ◑ The Golden Gate Bridge, San Francisco, USA

◐ ◑ The Grand Palace, Bangkok, Thailand

◐ ◑ The Canals and Belfry of Bruges, Belgium

◐ ◑ The city of Lhasa and the Potala Palace, Tibet, China

◐ ◑ Mount Everest, Nepal

◐ ◑ The White House, Washington, USA

Bucket *Done it*

○ ○ Iguazu Falls, Brazil/Argentina

○ ○ Ayers Rock, Australia

○ ○ Mount Rushmore National Memorial, South Dakota, USA

○ ○ Dome of the Rock, Jerusalem

○ ○ Mount Fuji, Japan

○ ○ Victoria Falls, Zimbabwe

○ ○ Sacre Coeur, Paris, France

○ ○ The Amazon Rainforest, Brazil

○ ○ Hermitage Museum, St. Petersburg, Russia

○ ○ Buddhist Temple, Angkor Wat, Cambodia

○ ○ The Eiffel Tower, Paris, France

○ ○ The Great Wall of China, China

○ ○ Temples of Borobudur, Indonesia

○ ○ Mont Saint-Michel, Brittany/Normandy, France

○ ○ Opera House, Sydney, Australia

○ ○ The Palace of Versailles, France

Bucket *Done it*

○ ○ Yosemite Park, California, USA

○ ○ Alhambra Palace, Grenada, Spain

○ ○ The Maoi Stone Monolith Figures, Easter Island

○ ○ The Blue Lagoon, South West of Reykjavik, Iceland

○ ○ Banff National Park, Canadian Rockies, Canada

○ ○ Jasper National Park, Canada

○ ○ The Winter Palace, St Petersburg, Russia

○ ○ Grand Bazaar, Istanbul, Turkey

○ ○ Abu Simbel Temples, Aswan Governorate, Egypt

○ ○ Moulin Rouge, Paris, France

○ ○ Windsor Castle, Windsor, England

○ ○ Grand Palace, Brussels, Belgium

○ ○ Kruger National Park, South Africa

○ ○ Copacabana Beach, Rio de Janeiro, Brazil

○ ○ Amber Palace, Rajastjan, India

○ ○ Tivoli Gardens, Copenhagen, Sweden

THE NEW 7 WONDERS OF THE WORLD

GREAT WALL OF CHINA
China 700BC

CHRIST THE REDEEMER
Rio de Janeiro, Brazil AD1931

PETRA MA'AN
Jordan 312BC

COLOSSEUM
Rome, Italy AD80

CHICHEN ITZA
Yucatan, Mexico AD600

MACHU PICCHU
Cuzco Region, Peru
AD1450

TAJ MAHAL
Agra, Uttar Pradesh, India
AD1643

THE WONDERS OF NATURE

Roll up, roll up. See them before they go. Last chance to see.
Witness nature, before it's just a fuzzy memory. All of these things
are fragile. All of them are in danger. Maybe a direct personal
experience will light the fire in you, set you off on a new path.
Or a vision of a mighty polar bear walking free, might be
something to tell the grandchildren one day. I saw them,
out there in the wild places, before they disappeared.

See a Komodo Dragon in Indonesia

Watch Giant Tortoises on the Galapagos Islands

Look out for Piranhas in Brazil

Spot Hippos in Bostswana

Witness the Wildebeest Migration – Serengeti
Tanzania/Maasai Mara Kenya

Spot Gorillas in Rwanda/Uganda

Track Lions in Kenya

Look for Elephants in Kenya

View Sea Turtles in Costa Rica

Go whale watching in South Africa

Bucket

Done it

○ ○ See Meerkats in Botswana

○ ○ View Orangutans in Indonesia

○ ○ Look for Zebra in Botswana

○ ○ See Camels in the Sahara, Morocco

○ ○ Spot a Sloth in Costa Rica

○ ○ Look out for Whale Sharks in Mozambique

○ ○ Watch Penguins in South Africa

○ ○ Study kangaroos in Australia

○ ○ Track Cheetahs in South Africa

○ ○ See Bears in Alaska

○ ○ Travel to see Leopards in Sri Lanka

○ ○ Study Koalas in Australia

○ ○ Watch Polar Bears in Canada

○ ○ Be captivated by Llamas in Peru

○ ○ View the Pandas of Chengdu, China

EPIC JOURNEYS

Read 'Zen & the Art of Motorcycle Maintenance'. Read 'On the Road'. Watch 'the Long Way Up', or any of a hundred other classic Epic Journeys. Then go and plan your own. If you think you can't afford it, get smart. 2007's 'Tuk tuk to the road' showed that two young women with no money could raise all the funding they needed to go around the world in a Tuk Tuk with the aid of a charitable cause and head for PR. Can you sell the book idea before you go? Even Che Guevara managed to get himself sponsored for his year out. (No word of a lie).

Drive the Pan-American Highway from Deadhorse Alaska to Puerto Montt in Chile

Walk El Camino de Santiago from France over the Pyrenees to the Spanish Cathedral Santiago de Compostela

Take the world's longest Train Journey: The Trans-Siberian Railway Moscow to Vladivostok

Travel the Sea to Sky Highway Canadian Highway 99 from Vancouver to Whistler

Trek the 37.3m Kepler Track roundtrip, South Island, New Zealand

Drive Coast to Coast across the USA: New York to Los Angeles

Bucket *Done it*

○ ○ Hike the Appalachian Trail, Georgia to Maine, USA

○ ○ Cruise Down the Yangtze River, Shanghai, China

○ ○ Sail down the Danube from Germany to the Black Sea

○ ○ Take on the Three Peaks Challenge, climbing the three highest peaks of Scotland, England and Wales

○ ○ Cycle from Canada to Mexico, down the West Coast of America

○ ○ Discover the stunning nature in a Drive from Grand Teton to Yellowstone, Wyoming, USA

○ ○ Climb to Base Camp, Everest

○ ○ Travel the Silk Road in the footsteps of Marco Polo, from Venice to China

○ ○ Drive the Pacific Coast Highway, California, USA

○ ○ Whitewater Raft down the Colorado, USA

○ ○ Cruise the Norwegian Fjords

Bucket *Done it*

○ ○ Ride the Rocky Mountaineer train from Colorado to Utah

○ ○ Trek the Atlas Mountains, Morocco

○ ○ Cycle from John O'Groats in Scotland to Land's End in England

○ ○ Follow in the footsteps of the British aristocracy by going on a Grand Tour across Europe

○ ○ Sail down the Ganges, India

○ ○ Walk the The Patagonian epic: Laguna de los Tres, Los Glaciares, Argentina

○ ○ Experience West Africa by train from Dakar in Senegal to Bamako in Mali

○ ○ Drive the Transfagarasan Highway in Romania

○ ○ Cross the Bolivian Salt Flats, Southwest Bolivia

○ ○ Sail down the Mekong River, Laos, Cambodia and Vietnam

○ ○ Cruise down the Nile from Luxor to Aswan, Egypt

Bucket
Done it

◯ ◯ Go backpacking through Europe

◯ ◯ Drive a campervan round the tip of Scotland
following the North Coast 500

◯ ◯ Travel round the world

◯ ◯ Drink beer at Oktoberfest, Germany

◯ ◯ Trek the "Walkway of Death" rope and cable trail,
Caminito Dell Rey, Malaga, Spain

◯ ◯ Discover the Skeleton Coast on a drive across the
Namib Desert. Start – Lüderitz; end – Walvis Bay,
Namibia

◯ ◯ Descend 120m into the Thrihnukagigur Volcano,
Iceland

◯ ◯ Travel London to Venice on the Venice
Simplon-Orient-Express

◯ ◯ Backpack 24m Grand Canyon rim to rim,
Grand National Park, Arizona, USA

AROUND THE WORLD

So many places, so little time.

There are 195 UN recognised countries of the world plus two UN observer states (and Taiwan, China).

Bucket *Done it*

- China
- India
- United States of America
- Indonesia
- Pakistan
- Brazil
- Nigeria
- Bangladesh
- Russia
- Japan
- Ethiopia
- Philippines
- Egypt
- DR Congo
- Turkey
- Iran
- Germany
- Thailand
- United Kingdom
- France

Bucket *Done it*

- Italy
- Tanzania
- South Africa
- Myanmar
- Kenya
- South Korea
- Colombia
- Spain
- Uganda
- Argentina
- Algeria
- Sudan
- Ukraine
- Iraq
- Afghanistan
- Poland
- Canada
- Morocco
- Saudi Arabia
- Uzbekistan
- Peru

Bucket	Done it		Bucket	Done it	
◯	◯	Angola	◯	◯	Chad
◯	◯	Malaysia	◯	◯	Somalia
◯	◯	Mozambique	◯	◯	Zimbabwe
◯	◯	Ghana	◯	◯	Guinea
◯	◯	Yemen	◯	◯	Rwanda
◯	◯	Nepal	◯	◯	Benin
◯	◯	Venezuela	◯	◯	Burundi
◯	◯	Madagascar	◯	◯	Tunisia
◯	◯	Cameroon	◯	◯	Bolivia
◯	◯	Code d'Ivoire	◯	◯	Belgium
◯	◯	North Korea	◯	◯	Haiti
◯	◯	Australia	◯	◯	Cuba
◯	◯	Niger	◯	◯	South Sudan
◯	◯	Sri Lanka	◯	◯	Dominican Republic
◯	◯	Burkina Faso	◯	◯	Czech Republic
◯	◯	Mali	◯	◯	Greece
◯	◯	Romania	◯	◯	Jordan
◯	◯	Malawi	◯	◯	Portugal
◯	◯	Chile	◯	◯	Azerbaijan
◯	◯	Kazakhstan	◯	◯	Sweden
◯	◯	Zambia	◯	◯	Honduras
◯	◯	Guatemala	◯	◯	United Arab Emirates
◯	◯	Ecuador	◯	◯	Hungary
◯	◯	Syria	◯	◯	Tajikistan
◯	◯	Netherlands	◯	◯	Belarus
◯	◯	Senegal	◯	◯	Austria
◯	◯	Cambodia	◯	◯	Papua New Guinea

Bucket   Done it

- Serbia
- Israel
- Switzerland
- Togo
- Sierra Leone
- Laos
- Paraguay
- Bulgaria
- Libya
- Lebanon
- Nicaragua
- Kyrgystan
- El Salvador
- Turkmenistan
- Singapore
- Denmark
- Finland
- Congo
- Slovakia
- Norway
- Oman
- State of Palestine
- Costa Rica
- Liberia
- Ireland
- Central African Republic

Bucket   Done it

- New Zealand
- Mauritania
- Panama
- Kuwait
- Croatia
- Moldova
- Georgia
- Eritrea
- Uruguay
- Bosnia and Herzegovina
- Mongolia
- Armenia
- Jamaica
- Qatar
- Albania
- Lithuania
- Namibia
- Gambia
- Botswana
- Gabon
- Lesotho
- North Macedonia
- Slovenia
- Guinea-Bissau
- Latvia
- Bahrain

Bucket	Done it		Bucket	Done it	
○	○	Equatorial Guinea	○	○	Sao Tome & Principe
○	○	Trinidad and Tobago	○	○	Samoa
			○	○	Saint Lucia
○	○	Estonia	○	○	Kirabati
○	○	Timor-Leste	○	○	Grenada
○	○	Mauritius	○	○	St Vincent & Grenadines
○	○	Cyprus			
○	○	Eswatini	○	○	Tonga
○	○	Djibouti	○	○	Seychelles
○	○	Fiji	○	○	Antigua and Barbuda
○	○	Comoros	○	○	Andorra
○	○	Guyana	○	○	Dominica
○	○	Bhutan	○	○	Marshall Islands
○	○	Solomon Islands	○	○	Saint Kitts & Nevis
○	○	Montenegro	○	○	Monaco
○	○	Luxembourg	○	○	Liechtenstein
○	○	Suriname	○	○	San Marino
○	○	Cabo Verde	○	○	Palau
○	○	Micronesia	○	○	Tuvalu
○	○	Maldives	○	○	Nauru
○	○	Malta	○	○	Holy See (Vatican city-state)
○	○	Brunei			
○	○	Belize	○	○	Taiwan, China
○	○	Bahamas			
○	○	Iceland			
○	○	Vanuatu			
○	○	Barbados			

ART AND CULTURE

People make some amazing things. You'll never regret going to see them. Scrolling through the twenty 'most amazing pieces of art ever' on the internet will never hit you the same way. Place and presence still mean something. Have an unmediated experience. But probs get a selfie with Michelangelo's David at the same time though yeah.

○ ○ See Antony Gormley's Another Place at Crosby Beach, Liverpool, England

○ ○ Marvel at The Girl with a Pearl Earring, The Hague, Netherlands

○ ○ Watch a play on Broadway, New York, USA

○ ○ See The Mona Lisa in The Louvre, Paris, France

○ ○ Catch a West End Musical in London, England

○ ○ Visit Monet's Garden in Giverny, France

○ ○ Get tickets for Glastonbury Music Festival, Worthy Farm, England

○ ○ Visit Michaelangelo's David, Florence, Tuscany, Italy

○ ○ Celebrate Dival, the Festival in Lights, India

○ ○ Go see The Terracotta Army, Lintong District, Xi'An, China

Bucket *Done it*

◯ ◯ Watch an Opera at Milan's Teatro all Scala

◯ ◯ Take in a country music performance at The Grand Ole Opry, Nashville, Tennessee

◯ ◯ Check out the Wynwood Walls street art district in Miami, Florida, USA

◯ ◯ Watch an Opera at Teatro La Fenice, Venice, Italy

◯ ◯ See a performance at The Edinburgh Festival, Edinburgh, Scotland

◯ ◯ Take in a play at The Globe Theatre, London, England

◯ ◯ See Peggy Guggenheim's art collection at her museum in Venice, Italy

◯ ◯ Don a mask at the Venice Carnival, Venice, Italy

◯ ◯ Have a Guinness on St. Patrick's Day, Dublin, Ireland

◯ ◯ Samba at Rio Carnival, Rio de Janeiro, Brazil

◯ ◯ Party at Mardi Gras, New Orleans, Louisanna, USA

◯ ◯ Find yourself at Burning Man, Black Rock Desert, Pershing County, Nevada, USA

MUSEUMS

Few things are more brilliant than a brilliant museum. Real memories are made in these fabulous cathedrals of knowledge and experience. Imagine yourself into other lives, other times. Get a sense of history, because we're all going to need it in the years to come. Don't forget to exit through the gift shop!

Bring us back a pencil.

Bucket *Done it*

- The Rijksmuseum, Amsterdam, The Netherlands

- The Prado, Madrid, Spain

- MOMA, New York, USA

- The Smithsonian Institution, Washington DC, USA

- The State Hermitage Museum, St Petersberg, Russia

- The Uffizi Galleries, Florence, Italy

- The British Museum, London, England

- The Grand Egyptian Museum, Cairo, Egypt

- The Metropolitan Museum of Art, New York, USA

- The National Archaeological Museum, Athens

- The Louvre, Paris, France

- The Tate Modern, London, England

- Museo Nacional de Antropologia, Mexico City, Mexico

Bucket
Done it

- Musee D'Orsay, Paris, France
- Museo Nacional Del Prado, Madrid, Spain
- The National Gallery, London, England
- The Van Gogh Museum, Amsterdam, Netherlands
- Galleria dell'Accademia, Florence, Italy
- Pergamon Museum, Berlin, Germany
- Vatican Museums, Vatican City, Italy
- National Museum of China, Beijing, China
- National History Museum, London, England
- American Museum of Natural History, New York
- Victoria and Albert Museum, London, England
- National Palace Museum, Taipei, Taiwan, China
- National Museum of African American History and Culture, Washington DC
- Museum of Qin Terractotta Warriors and Horse, Xi'an, China
- Museo Nacional de Antropologia, Mexico City, Mexico
- Centre Georges-Pompidou, Paris, France

Coca Cola in USA

Irn Bru in Scotland

Vodka in Russia

Gin in England

Beer in Belgium

Rum in Cuba

DRINK IT IN...

Feni in Goa, India

Irish Whiskey in Ireland

Prosecco in Italy

Ouzo in Greece

Port in Portugal

Cava in Spain

Sangria in Spain

Scotch Whisky in Scotland

Champagne in France

Tea in China

Pilsner in Czech Republic

Tequila in Mexico

DRINK IT IN...

Lager in Germany

Bubble Tea in Taiwan, China

Guinness in Ireland

Espresso in Italy

Red Wine in France

FILM AND TV LOCATIONS

Have you ever wandered around New York? Ever get the feeling you've been there before? Try not to trip over the film crews. Some places exist almost more vividly in our collective imagination than they do in reality. Places where the dream world of storytelling has changed the real world in some subtle and powerful way. Like Bram Stoker did for Transylvania (and Whitby), these places are now half-real at best.

You will have your own such places, from the stories that you connected with the most, not always from mass market commercial hits. Make your own version of this list...

- **The Sound of Music:** Singing 'The Hills Are Alive' to The Sound of Music, Salzberg, The Austrian Tyrol, Austria

- **Dolce Vita:** Throw a coin into the Trevi Fountain, Rome, Italy

- **Lawrence of Arabia:** Wadi Rum, Aqaba, Jordan

- **When Harry Met Sally:** Katz's Delicatessen, New York, USA

- **The Godfather:** Savoca and Forza D'agro, Sicily, Italy

- **The Warriors:** Take a subway train to Coney Island, New York, USA

- **Ghostbusters:** New York Public Library, New York, USA

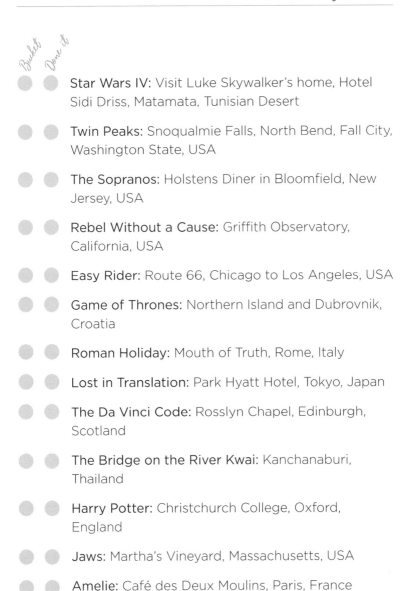

Star Wars IV: Visit Luke Skywalker's home, Hotel Sidi Driss, Matamata, Tunisian Desert

Twin Peaks: Snoqualmie Falls, North Bend, Fall City, Washington State, USA

The Sopranos: Holstens Diner in Bloomfield, New Jersey, USA

Rebel Without a Cause: Griffith Observatory, California, USA

Easy Rider: Route 66, Chicago to Los Angeles, USA

Game of Thrones: Northern Island and Dubrovnik, Croatia

Roman Holiday: Mouth of Truth, Rome, Italy

Lost in Translation: Park Hyatt Hotel, Tokyo, Japan

The Da Vinci Code: Rosslyn Chapel, Edinburgh, Scotland

The Bridge on the River Kwai: Kanchanaburi, Thailand

Harry Potter: Christchurch College, Oxford, England

Jaws: Martha's Vineyard, Massachusetts, USA

Amelie: Café des Deux Moulins, Paris, France

Bucket *Done it*

○ ○ **Notting Hill:** Portobello Road Market, The Notting Hill Bookshop, London, England

○ ○ **Downton Abbey:** Highclere Castle, Highclere, Newbury, West Berkshire, England

○ ○ **Lord of the Rings:** Matamata, North Island, New Zealand

○ ○ **The Shining:** Timberline Lodge, Mount Hood, Oregon, USA

○ ○ **The Good, The Bad and The Ugly:** Tabernas Desert, Andalucia, Spain

○ ○ **Mamma Mia!:** Skopelos Church of Agios Ioannis Kastri, Greece

○ ○ **Close Encounters of the Third Kind:** Devils Tower, Wyoming USA

○ ○ **Forest Gump:** The Bench at Chippewa Square, Savannah, Georgia, USA

○ ○ **Breakfast at Tiffany's:** Tiffany's, New York, USA

○ ○ **Rocky:** Run up the 68 steps of the Philadelphia Museum of Art, Philadelphia, USA

○ ○ . . . and re-watch the movie I loved as a child

GO CLIMB A MOUNTAIN

Let's get higher. It's time for your ascension. All you have to do is put one foot in front of the other. Let the imperceptible movement of the tectonic plates gently push your body and mind way up out of the valley of everyday life. The world still is beautiful, and always was.

Bucket *Done it*

Mount Kilimanjaro, Tanzania 5,895 m

Mount Whitney, California, USA 4,421 m

Mount Fuji, Japan 3,776 m

Mount Rainier, Washington State, USA 4,392 m

Mount Kosciuszko, Australia 2,228 m

Pikes Peak, Colorado, USA 4,302 m

Ben Nevis, Lochaber, Scotland 1,345 m

Mount Kosciuszko, Thredbo, Australia 2,228 m

Mauna Kea, Hawaii, USA 4,207 m

Mount Baker, Washington State, USA 3,286 m

Snowdon, Snowdonia, Wales 1,085 m

Mount Temple, Canada 3,544 m

Mount Toubkal, Morocco 4,167 m

Mount Triglav, Slovenia 2,864 m

Everest 8,849 m (even if its just base camp 5,364m)

FOOD

So many people travel with their stomachs there is an entire
category of books called 'food travel' and apparently
'food explorer' is a profession now. Get thinking!
How can you blag sponsorship to go and eat the world?
Food travel influencer? Cruise ship chef?

Bucket *Done it*

Eat Pizza in Naples, Italy

Have Irish Stew in Dublin, Ireland

Eat Fish and Chips at the seaside in England

Sample Tapas in Seville, Spain

Try Gumbo in New Orleans, Louisiana, USA

Savour a Crepe with honey in Paris, France

Eat Goulash in Budapest, Hungary

Have a Wiener Schnitzel in Vienna, Austria

Sample Moules-frites in Brussels, Belgium

Eat Peking Duck in Peking, China

Have Swedish Meatballs in Stockholm, Sweden

Feast on Fried Pork with Rice and Beans in Haiti

Have a hamburger in USA

Bucket Done it

○ ○ Eat a traditional Roast Beef Dinner in London, England

○ ○ Eat Moussaka in Athens, Greece

○ ○ Eat a deep-fried Mars Bar in Glasgow, Scotland

○ ○ Eat Pad Thai in Bangkok, Thailand

○ ○ Have a Curry in Mumbai, India

○ ○ Eat a Philly Cheese Steak in Philadelphia, USA

○ ○ Have a Felafel in Jerusalem, Israel

○ ○ Sample Sushi in Tokyo, Japan

○ ○ Have a Doner Kebab in Turkey

○ ○ Eat Cou Cou and Flying Fish in Barbados

○ ○ Enjoy a Taco in Mexico City, Mexico

○ ○ Sample Dim Sum in Hong Kong, China

○ ○ Eat food cooked in a Tagine, in Tangiers, Morocco

○ ○ Have Haggis in Edinburgh, Scotland

○ ○ Sample Paella in Barcelona, Spain

○ ○ Tuck into Poutine, Quebec, Canada

CLASSIC BOOK LOCATIONS AND INSPIRATIONS

Who can pass by Baker Street in London without a shiver of delight? Books are better than everything and recent studies have proved it. A UCL study found that listening to audiobooks was more emotionally engaging than watching films or TV shows. Not only that, readers understand other people's emotions better. Finding the places where great books were set, or places that inspired great books is a really fun way to travel.

Consider it a modern pilgrimage.

Harry Potter by J. K. Rowling
Alnwick Castle | Northumberland, England
Glenfinnan Viaduct, Lochaber, Scotland
King's Cross Station | London, England:
Platform 9¾:

Wuthering Heights by Emily Brontë
Top Withens, Haworth, Yorkshire Moors: 16th century farmhouse

Ulysees by James Joyce
Martello Tower, Sandy Cove. This spot is now home to The James Joyce Tower and Museum, Dublin

Bucket *Done it*

The Talented Mr Ripley by Patricia Highsmith
The beautiful island of Ischia, Bay of Naples, Italy:
The fictional resort of 'Mongibello'
Ca' Sagredo Hotel, Venice: Ripley's apartment
Café Florian, Piazza San Marco: Marge voices her
suspicions about Dickie's disappearance

Dracula by Dram Stoker
The novel begins in Transylvania, Romania at Bran
Castle, then moves to Whitby, Yorkshire, England

The Great Gatsby by F. Scott Fitzgerald
Sands Point, Long Island, New York inspired the
East Egg house
Execution Rocks Lighthouse that calls out to
Gatsby, drawing him closer to this long lost love
Daisy.

The Da Vinci Code by Dan Brown
Rosslyn Chapel, Roslin, near Edinburgh, Scotland:
the centre of a conspiracy theory in the book.

Lord of the Rings by JRR Tolkien
Forest of Dean, Gloucestershire, England: inspired
by the rolling hills and lush trees. Also Moseley
Bog, the marsh behind his childhood home.

Bucket *Done it*

○ ○ **The Spy Who Came In From The Cold
by John le Carre**
Berlin: an important muse for many novelist and
easy to see why Le Carre was captivated to
imagine his Cold War thriller based here.

○ ○ **Death On The Nile by Agatha Christie**
Cairo, Egypt: Poirot is sent to solve the murder of
Linnet Ridgeway aboard a night boat on the Nile.

○ ○ **A Room With A View by E. M. Forster**
Florence, Italy: A story of Edwardian English
society governed by strict Victorian values.

○ ○ **To Kill A Mocking Bird by Harper Lee**
Maycomb, Alabama is a fictional city but based on
Lee's childhood home and experiences of
Monroeville, Alabama.

○ ○ **Bleak House by Charles Dickens**
Broadstairs, Kent: the cliff house where Charles
Dickens used to spend his summer holidays which
inspired his novel.

○ ○ **Winnie the Pooh by A.A. Milne**
Ashdown Forest, East Sussex: inspired the
Hundred Acre Wood and illustrator E. H. Shepard
also used the forest for inspiration while bringing
the story to life.

Bucket

Done it

Ode To A Nightingale by John Keats
The Spaniards Inn, London, England: inspired
Keats while listening to birds in the inn's garden.
The location is also mentioned in Charles Dickens's
The Pickwick Papers and Bram Stoker's Dracula.

The Catcher in the Rye by J. D.Salinger
"The Pond" at Central Park, New York City: Holden
Caulfield contemplates where all the ducks go.

Wild by Cheryl Strayed
The Pacific Crest Train, USA: a three month trek in
an attempt to heal herself from the loss of her
mother.

Romeo and Juliet by William Shakespeare
Verona, Italy: Branded The City Of Love, Juliet's
house that belonged to the Dal Cappello family
(The Capulets) features the famous balcony where
you can stand and relive the scene.

Heidi by Johanna Spyri
Maienfeld, Switzerland

Jane Eyre by Charlotte Bronte
Norton Conyers, Ripon, Yorkshire, England: The
Manor House was the fictional Thornfield Hall
which inspired the character or Mrs Rochester in
the novel.

THE BIG 50

The locations you might see in a James Bond movie, they're all chosen because everybody in the world wants to visit them, and they're right to. If you even managed to hit half a dozen of these locations, you'd have seen enough of the great seething, luscious, filthy variety of human built environments to remind you to approach this life with the sense of awe that it deserves.

We are living in such strange and massive colonies of monkey ants clinging to a rock in a void, and any view of the world that forgets this point is missing something.

Bucket　Done it

⬤　⬤　Saint Tropez, France

⬤　⬤　Dubrovnik, Croatia

⬤　⬤　Bethlehem, Palestine

⬤　⬤　Jerusalem Old City, Israel

⬤　⬤　Marrakech, Morocco

⬤　⬤　Paris, France

⬤　⬤　Berlin, Germany

⬤　⬤　London, England

⬤　⬤　Edinburgh, Scotland

Bucket Done it

○ ○ Stockholm, Sweden

○ ○ St Petersberg, Russia

○ ○ New York, USA

○ ○ Los Angeles, USA

○ ○ Dublin, Ireland

○ ○ Barcelona, Spain

○ ○ Madrid, Spain

○ ○ Rome, Italy

○ ○ Venice, Italy

○ ○ Shanghai, China

○ ○ Melbourne, Australia

○ ○ Milan, Italy

○ ○ Athens, Greece

○ ○ Moscow, Russia

Bucket Done it

⬤ ⬤ Bangkok, Thailand

⬤ ⬤ Cairo, Egypt

⬤ ⬤ Vienna, Austria

⬤ ⬤ Las Vegas, USA

⬤ ⬤ Ho Chi Minh City, Vietnam

⬤ ⬤ Mexico City, Mexico

⬤ ⬤ Osaka, Japan

⬤ ⬤ Lisbon, Portugal

⬤ ⬤ Miami, USA

⬤ ⬤ Agra, India

⬤ ⬤ Tokyo, Japan

⬤ ⬤ Kuala Lumpur, Malaysia

⬤ ⬤ Amsterdam, Netherlands

⬤ ⬤ Seoul, South Korea

Bucket   Done it

○ ○ Prague, Czech Republic

○ ○ Guangzhou, China

○ ○ Taipei, Taiwan, China

○ ○ Rio de Janeiro, Brazil

○ ○ Mumbai, India

○ ○ Beijing, China

○ ○ Delhi, India

○ ○ Istanbul, Turkey

○ ○ Havana, Cuba

○ ○ Dubai, UAE

○ ○ Singapore, Singapore

○ ○ Buenos Aires, Argentina

○ ○ Vancouver, Canada

"
my adventures

DREAM
LIST
"

In a world of limitless possibility, which of these adventures would you choose? Forget about reality. Choose from the suggestions on the previous pages and alter, combine, remix, and expand.

Fill these pages. Don't think. Just dream.

my adventures

TASK LIST

Go back through your dream list and choose one actionable first step for each item.

The dream does not become reality, on it's journey toward reality it becomes something else.

experiences

HAVE GREAT TIMES

Experiences are often a reward for us expanding our perception of who we are to include something new.

As Seth Godin recently identified, the secret question we often ask ourselves before we do something is this 'Do people like me do things like this?'

Identity can be fun, but it can also hold you back. So, when you browse this cacophony of trials and ordeals and concoct your own personal twelve trials of Hercules, consider this - add some experiences that 'people like you wouldn't do'.

I bet you the head of a medusa in a bag that those'll be the most powerful experiences you have.

Next time you find yourself in the shower, try this. Turn the temperature down just a little bit. Breathe and adapt. Now repeat this process, little by little. Get as far as you can towards the cold, but breathing slow and easy all the time. Not so fast that you start to gasp.

Gasping must be avoided.

Now when you've gone as far as you can, flip the tap all the way over to cold and try to stay under for ten seconds. You can breathe deeply. You can rub your body with your hands to distract you from the panic, but try your best to hold for ten seconds.

You might find that you break through the panic and into a new state of being at peace with the cold. Probably not though. It'll probably be awful, and you'll leap out of the water as soon as you can. But you'll notice every minute detail of how it feels. You'll be 100% in the present moment for a few seconds.

And you'll feel like an absolute badass for even having tried, even if you failed.

This is our baseline definition of an experience. In the 'Hero's Journey' these would be 'Trials' or even more traditionally 'Ordeals'. If an adventure is a whole story, an experience is a scene.

An experience happens when you cross a threshold. The threshold is often guarded by a monster. In this case, your ancient primal fear of freezing to death. These days the monster is often your ancient primal fear of being laughed at and despised by your tribe.

MY EXPERIENCES

Are you experienced? People want experiences. More and more studies have shown. A 2019 study found more than three quarters of respondents preferred to spend money on experiences than commodities. In particular, they say millennials prefer buying new experiences to buying new things.

Experiences can be an escape from an everyday life that leaves many of us feeling trapped and deprived of meaning. The old narrative of building a career and buying a house and having a nuclear family seems out of reach for the next generation. Work is a series of meaningless gigs. Social life has been turned into another form of paid work. Everybody has a side hustle. Life is hard work, albeit in a very different way.

An experience can take us away from all this. We can leave our normality to have a laugh and have fun with people. But we can also seek experiences to learn something new, not necessarily for some predefined economic advantage. Learning something for the fun of it is very different to doing that course at work.

A massive amount of people seek new experiences as an escape from anxiety.

Small wonder, these are anxious times. The mental health epidemic in the West is well documented. We seek experiences that will reduce our anxiety and free us from chronic stress. Whether that might be a cathartic outburst or a meditation retreat, depends on you.

We also seek meaning from our experiences. We want to respond to the environmental crisis, to get involved in some meaningful way. And the opportunities are out there, from volunteering on organic farms to beach cleans.

"

The carnival of life. The rich tapestry. The buffet of sensory experience. If you have not eaten Escamol (fried ants), have you ever really lived?

"

"

*adrenalin
hunter*

"

Danger. Those of us lucky enough to be seeking it are those of us who rarely ever experience it. Some of us have had the incredible fortune of being born into the least dangerous parts of a world which is generally less dangerous for humans than ever in history.

The problem is, we evolved to experience long periods of calm punctuated by sporadic moments of intense risk. Now we experience a kind of self-induced and near constant state of mild fear. We call it chronic stress. We traded moments of real violence for a life of imaginary impending dooms, the fear of running out of money, of not paying the bills, of losing status, of being thrown out of the tribe to starve.

Sometimes a short sharp shock can snap us out of worrying ourselves to death about all that fake danger.

There is something deeply cathartic about experiencing the fight or flight reflex in its full glory. We have perhaps a secret inner nostalgia for occasionally being chased by sabre tooth tigers.

Adrenaline, or epinephrine if you're showing off, gets dumped into your system by the adrenal medulla, causing your body to enter fight or flight mode. You get an extra boost of glucose from the reserves, your air passages dilate to allow oxygen to flood the muscles, your sensitivity to pain is dialled down and your awareness and performance get a sudden boost. It's intense. It's strangely more-ish.

And when you face the fear and do it anyway, you gain a new confidence to take with you back into your everyday life.

Who knows, you might even find it a little easier to put your everyday stresses into perspective.

Go deep sea sport fishing

Do a sky dive

Try parkour

Go hang gliding

Go heli-skiing

Go snowboarding

Do a bungee jump

Go kite surfing

ADRENALINE EXPERIENCES

Try zorbing

Go surfing

Go cage diving with sharks

Shoot a gun

Go powerboat racing

Try zip lining

Go caving

Experience paragliding

Try land surfing

Go rock climbing

Go rally driving

Fly in a microlight

Learn to waterski

Experience kite boarding or land boarding

Try canyoning

Go skiing

ADRENALINE EXPERIENCES

Try wakeboarding

Do a cliff dive/jump

Go white water rafting

Do a race-track day

Go snowmobile riding

Ride a jet ski

Try base jumping

SEIZE THE DAY

What makes an experience? Two ingredients: risk & investment.
Some have hopes and dreams, you've got ways and means.
You've been talking that talk, now get walking that walk! **Carpe**
the frak out of that **diem** you bloody legend!

Bucket *Done it*

Witness a solar eclipse

Take a ride in a hot air balloon

See an event at the Olympics

Get a tattoo

Get a piercing

Make my own wine

Take flying lessons

Go to a masked ball

Go paddle boarding

Fly first class

Respond to a random personal ad

Return to my childhood school

Bucket   Done it

○ ○   Be a movie extra

○ ○   Act in a play

○ ○   Bet at a casino

○ ○   Go deep sea fishing

○ ○   Hit an archery bulls-eye

○ ○   Ride a horse

○ ○   Perform on a stage

○ ○   Take my grandparents somewhere special

○ ○   Attend an NBL/NFL/NHL game

○ ○   Attend a Premiership/La Liga/Bundesliga/Serie A game

○ ○   Go cage diving with sharks

○ ○   Go speed-dating

○ ○   Go to a music festival

○ ○   Have afternoon tea at The Ritz, London

○ ○   Start a collection

Bucket   Done it

○ ○   Quit my job

○ ○   Take a cookery class

○ ○   Go stargazing

○ ○   Sign up for voluntary work

○ ○   Send a message in a bottle

○ ○   Start a scrapbook

○ ○   Learn to ride a motorbike

○ ○   Master a magic trick

○ ○   Start a YouTube channel

○ ○   Make my own beer

○ ○   Get fitted for an item of made to measure of clothing

○ ○   Organize a family portrait

○ ○   Give a hitchhiker a lift

○ ○   Ask for a sabbatical and take a month off work

○ ○   Date someone 20 years older than me

Bucket Done it

○ ○ Make an item of clothing that I can wear

○ ○ Get two friends together and go on a special vacation

○ ○ Go on a wellness retreat

○ ○ Join a book club

○ ○ Have my palm read

○ ○ Have a tarot reading

○ ○ Charter a yacht

○ ○ Fly in a private jet

○ ○ Be part of a TV studio audience

○ ○ Dive the world's largest sinkhole, The Great Blue Hole, Belize

○ ○ Swim in The Devil's Pool, Victoria Falls, Zambia/Zimbabwe

○ ○ Watch The Running of the Bulls, Pamplona, Spain

○ ○ Hit a bullseye in darts

"
shoot for
the moon
"

What if the sky were the limit?

What if there were no limits?

What would you do if you could do anything?

As we mature, we learn the art of the possible. It's necessary of course. If you shoot for the moon you usually miss, and most days you can't afford to miss.

But when you get the hang of keeping yourself alive, maybe it's time to start staring up at that big old moon again from time to time. Because after all, everything really interesting in human history starts with someone saying something like 'Hey, what if we could fly?' Or 'What if we could create a bacteria that eats plastic?', or 'What if the world was round?'

Maybe nowadays the most radical what if questions might be negative.

'What if we could all stop flying?' or 'What if we could have an economic model that is not based on infinite growth?' or 'What if we could try out not being ruled by the whims of eccentric billionaires?'

So, what's your moon shot? If the stars aligned and you saw the chance to do something utterly historic, what would it be?

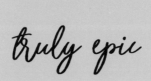

truly epic

Sometimes the stars align and the plans come together and you get the chance to do something TRULY EPIC.

The secret about truly epic plans is that sometimes it is easier to do something UNBELIEVABLE than it is to do something fairly ordinary.

This is partly because it's much easier to get people interested in HELPING YOU TO ACHIEVE a plan if that plan is VERY VERY EXCITING.

Witness the number of people who have managed to blag funding to go on incredible journeys by pitching it as a book idea first.

All you need is a fresh angle. Get your pirate crew together and start brainstorming!

Here's a few ideas to get you started...

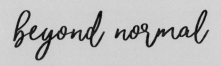

beyond normal

Here we take a look at the art of the impossible.

Here are some goals for your Bucket List that most people would never even attempt.

Not for the faint of heart...

MMM... THIS MIGHT TAKE SOME TIME

TRAVEL INTO SPACE

RUN THE MARATHON DES SABLES, SAHARA DESERT

GO ROUND THE WORLD IN 80 DAYS

START A BUSINESS THAT GOES ON TO TURNOVER A MILLION $

GIVE AWAY ALL MY EARTHLY POSSESSIONS

BREAK A WORLD RECORD

GO ON A DIVE TO SEE THE WRECKAGE OF THE TITANIC

CLEAR ALL OF MY DEBTS

COMPLETE AN IRONMAN TRIATHLON

CLIMB EVEREST

MEET THE QUEEN

BUILD MY OWN HOME

STUDY FOR A PHD

ROW THE ATLANTIC, SPAIN TO ANTIGUA

TREK THE 125M WALKER'S HAUTE ROUTE, FRENCH & SWISS ALPS

PRODUCE, WRITE OR DIRECT A MOVIE

FLY IN A WING SUITE

fun time

Adults need to play.

There are proper scientific studies to back this up. Play improves your brain and builds your creativity. It can help to heal emotional wounds. It can even improve your memory.

You need no excuses to go and have a muck about!

Stuart Brown, expert in play, wrote about five different types of fun time you should be packing into your adult life as often as you can.

Rough and tumble. Your health permitting, including all kinds of sports and just plain old scrapping with your kids or dog. Get out and start a game of rounders in the park. Have you got a frisbee? Why not?

Ritual play. Get out the old board games. Get out the new ones. We're living through a golden age of board game design, go check it out. Make that poker night happen. Join that chess club. Why not try role playing games?

Imaginative play. Join the local theatre group. Get doodling, colouring, writing stories. Everyone should have a craft. Everyone should try stand up comedy at least once. Try the local soul choir. Sing at an open mic night.

Body play. Any type of playful or creative use of the body from long walks to aerial yoga to circus skills to street dance.

Object play. Give me one good reason why you don't have a bucket of lego in your house. Manipulating stuff is awesome. Where is your toy box? What's in it? Get yourself some toys!

" What follows is a few suggestions for adventures where FUN is the priority. "

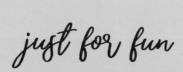

just for fun

Letting loose.

This section is all about
fun experiences.

Bucket   Done it

Run naked in the snow

Apply to be a contestant in a TV games show

Decide an important decision by flipping a coin

Flirt with someone

Sing karaoke to a room full of strangers

Kiss the Blarney Stone, Monacnapa, Ireland

Get a secret tattoo

Join the mile high club

Go on a blind date

Leave a note in a library book

Hire a sports car for a day

Send a message in a bottle

Dance in the rain

Enter a talent contest

Camp in the wilderness

Jump into a swimming pool fully clothed

Create an alter-ego and be that person for
24 hours

THE JOURNEY IS THE DESTINATION

You can fly from London to New York in five hours or you can do the crossing in two weeks on a cruise ship. Which one would you remember forever? Slow travel is back. Because getting the train from London to Rome is 1000% more romantic than flying and at least a degree more environmentally responsible. It bears repeating that the way you travel changes **the way you experience the destination.**

Bucket *Done it*

◯ ◯ Fly on a plane

◯ ◯ Travel by train

◯ ◯ Ski on skis

◯ ◯ Sail on a sail boat

◯ ◯ Ride in a Rolls Royce

◯ ◯ Ride on a horse

◯ ◯ Paddle a canoe

◯ ◯ Ride a zipline

◯ ◯ Go hiking

◯ ◯ Ride on a Segway

◯ ◯ Sail on a ferry

◯ ◯ Drive a supercar

◯ ◯ Fly in a helicopter

Bucket   Done it

◯ ◯   Paddle a kayak

◯ ◯   Ride on the subway

◯ ◯   Do a firewalk across hot coals

◯ ◯   Ride on a scooter

◯ ◯   Fly in a glider

◯ ◯   Ride on a jet ski

◯ ◯   Ride on an airboat

◯ ◯   Travel on a hovercraft

◯ ◯   Climb a mountain

◯ ◯   Sail in a submarine

◯ ◯   Fly in a hot air balloon

◯ ◯   Ride in a limo

◯ ◯   Sail on a cruise ship

◯ ◯   Ride on a motorcycle

◯ ◯   Drive in a dune buggy

◯ ◯   Ride a camel

◯ ◯   Ride on the back of a motorcycle

◯ ◯   Fly by private jet

◯ ◯   Sail on a catamaran

events

What is an event? A planned experience for a multitude of people to experience together. We are social animals and some of our most memorable and defining experiences come from those moments when we surrender our individuality to the group and become some kind of big uni-mind thing.

This could mean an intimate performance to a small crowd, or an epic festival event. Events are always an experience, and they always give you stories to tell. Who has ever forgotten a gig or a good party or that time they stumbled across an Easter parade in Guatemala City (OK that's one of mine). Events have the power to change us.

How many people have had a life changing revelation, a flash of inspiration at an event? How many of us have suddenly seen our lives in a new light and figured out a new direction in the midst of a festival of some kind or another?

Festivals. Carnivals. Ritual chaos. They have existed since the dawn of civilisation.
We need events.

Events took a beating during the first year of the pandemic, but they're back, different of course but they are back, at least for now. And if you don't feel ready to go back out to a massive stadium rave just yet, maybe you'll find some inspiration here for something smaller.

"We are the sum total of our experiences"
Dr. Gilovich

SPORTING PILGRIMAGES TO MAKE

Ever since the crowds went wild in the Colosseum of Ancient Rome, we have loved the electric atmosphere of watching feats of human prowess and virility, while surrendering our precious individuality to the glorious primal uni-mind of the baying mob. Few things in our sanitised modern world still inspire as much passion as these legendary sporting events...

Grand Sumo Wrestling Tournament in Japan

Le Tour de France cycle race, July, France

El Clasico Football match Barcelona vs Real Madrid, Spain

The Australian Open Tennis Tournament, Melbourne, Australia

The Indianapolis 500 car race at Indianapolis Motor Speedway in Indiana, USA

The Ashes Test Cricket series between England vs Australia

The Summer Olympic Games

The Winter Olympic Games

The All England Lawn Tennis Championships, Wimbledon, London, England

Bucket Done it

The New York City Marathon, New York, USA

The Argentinian Superclasico football game, Boca Juniors vs River Plate

The Ryder Cup Golf Competition between Europe and the USA held every two years alternating between USA and Europe

The Red Sox vs Yankees Major League Baseball game

The FIFA Football World Cup

The Derby horse race at Epsom, England

Polo at Palermo, Buenos Aires, Argentina

The FA Cup Final, Wembley, London, England

The Monaco Grand Prix, held in Monaco since 1929

The Grand National horse race at Aintree Racecourse in Liverpool, England

The Super Bowl, the annual championship game of the NFL

The Cricket World Cup

Bucket *Done it*

- ⚪ ⚪ The Copa Libertadores Football competition in South America

- ⚪ ⚪ The US Open Golf Tournament

- ⚪ ⚪ The 24 Hours of Le Mans, The oldest sports car endurance race in the world, near the town of Le Mans, France

- ⚪ ⚪ The All-Ireland Hurling Final, Dublin, Ireland

- ⚪ ⚪ The Golf Masters, Augusta, Georgia, USA

- ⚪ ⚪ The Tour of Italy cycle race, Italy

- ⚪ ⚪ The NBA Finals, USA

- ⚪ ⚪ The Davis Cup Tennis Competition

- ⚪ ⚪ The Rugby World Cup

- ⚪ ⚪ The National Hockey League, Stanley Finals

- ⚪ ⚪ The Daytona 500 NASCAR race, Daytona, Florida, USA

- ⚪ ⚪ The Kentucky Derby, Churchill Downs, Kentucky

- ⚪ ⚪ The Baseball World Series, USA

Bucket Done it

◯ ◯   The Highland Games, venues across Scotland

◯ ◯   The Rose Bowl, Pasadena, USA

◯ ◯   The London Marathon, London, England

◯ ◯   The MotoGP World Championship Motorcycle
       Race

◯ ◯   The Six Nations Rugby Championship

◯ ◯   The America's Cup the most prestigious sailing
       competition in the world

◯ ◯   The Football UEFA Champions League Final

◯ ◯   The British Open Golf Tournament, England and
       Scotland

◯ ◯   The Boston Marathon, Boston, Massachusetts, USA

◯ ◯   The Scottish old firm football derby Celtic vs
       Rangers, Glasgow, Scotland

◯ ◯   Isle of Man Motorcycle TT, Isle of Man, England

◯ ◯   The Tour of Spain cycle race, Spain

THINGS TO OWN

"Nice things make life nicer" Jack Black

And if you can't **own it** then, borrow it, rent it . . . find it second hand, buy the knock-off version or make your own. With a little ingenuity, many of these things are closer than you might think.

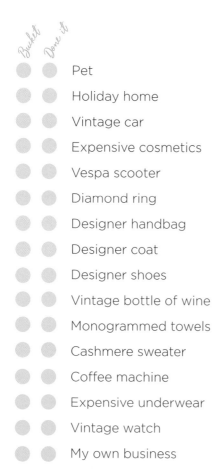

Bucket Done it

- Pet
- Holiday home
- Vintage car
- Expensive cosmetics
- Vespa scooter
- Diamond ring
- Designer handbag
- Designer coat
- Designer shoes
- Vintage bottle of wine
- Monogrammed towels
- Cashmere sweater
- Coffee machine
- Expensive underwear
- Vintage watch
- My own business

Bucket Done it

○ ○ A boat

○ ○ A plane

○ ○ A paddle board

○ ○ A bike

○ ○ All the classic novels I wish I'd read

○ ○ A convertible

○ ○ A round the world plane ticket

○ ○ Expensive Champagne

○ ○ Rare antiques

○ ○ Original art

○ ○ Solar panels

○ ○ Complete works of Shakespeare

○ ○ A tailored suit

○ ○ A life journal

○ ○ Season tickets

○ ○ A vintage campervan

○ ○ A high end sound system

○ ○ A hot tub

○ ○ A sauna

○ ○ Chickens

○ ○ ...and the one thing that I would really like to own

SLEEP

You can get the measure of a person from how many random places they have woken up. If you've never woken up on the kitchen floor, or on a park bench, have you really been living?

Here's a whole host of much classier, and probably safer places to lay your head.

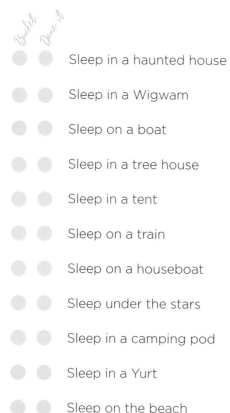

Bucket

Done it

Sleep in a haunted house

Sleep in a Wigwam

Sleep on a boat

Sleep in a tree house

Sleep in a tent

Sleep on a train

Sleep on a houseboat

Sleep under the stars

Sleep in a camping pod

Sleep in a Yurt

Sleep on the beach

Sleep underwater

Bucket   Done it

◯ ◯   Sleep in a capsule hotel

◯ ◯   Sleep in a caravan

◯ ◯   Sleep in a prison

◯ ◯   Sleep on an airplane

◯ ◯   Sleep in an ice hotel

◯ ◯   Sleep in a youth hostel

◯ ◯   Sleep in a Trulli

◯ ◯   Sleep in a cave

◯ ◯   Sleep in a motorhome

◯ ◯   Sleep underground

◯ ◯   Sleep in a shelter that I made

◯ ◯   Sleep on a couch

◯ ◯   Sleep in an airport

◯ ◯   Sleep on a waterbed

◯ ◯   Go a night without sleep

"my experiences

DREAM
LIST
"

In a world of limitless possibility, which of these experiences would you choose? Forget about reality. Choose from the suggestions on the previous pages and alter, combine, remix, and expand.

Fill these pages. Don't think. Just dream.

my experiences

TASK
LIST

Go back through your dream list and choose one actionable first step for each item.

The dream does not become reality, on it's journey toward reality it becomes something else.

growth

SELF IMPROVEMENT,
EXPRESSIONS
AND ACHIEVEMENTS

Anything you do for love and not money
is a revolutionary act.

What are the ingredients of an achievement? First take a big dose of delayed gratification. Then pour in a whole bunch of imperfect conditions and random obstacles. Add a good slug of self-doubt and stir it all up with a big dream and some good old fashioned grit.

Achievements start out with inspiration. The first time you hear someone, someone just like you speak another language, and it blows you away. A seed is planted. The strongest way to affect someone is to show them something you cannot fathom is possible.

Next comes fantasy. We imagine ourselves having some new superpower. Bending a shot into the corner of a goal, designing our own clothes, writing code, doing the splits or mixing the perfect cocktail. We imagine how happy we will be with this incredible new ability.

Then comes the fool, setting out merrily on a journey with no idea of what agonies may come. The honeymoon period begins. We throw ourselves at the new thing.

And now for the kung fu. Sustained effort over time. Sustained effort over time. Sustained effort over time. Banging your head against the wall. Plateau. Never mind. You cannot fail if you do not stop.

And then you break through.

There is no high like the breakthrough moment.

Achievements don't just make you feel awesome, they inspire other people to be more awesome. And now you have achieved something awesome, you can teach other people to do it too!

GROWTH AND ACHIEVEMENTS

Next time you find you are about to tell the world that you are terrible at something, shut the hell up and go and take time to improve it. You live in an age when anyone can teach themselves anything with fantastic free learning resources online. Give it ten hours. Test yourself at hour zero and at hour ten. Be amazed at how much progress you can make in ten hours.

Be unsatisfied with the status quo, go out to the woods in search of change, find a teacher, defeat your demons, win the treasure of progress and return to the village with a new skill and a story to tell. Learning is always a hero's journey. Growth and achievements are the badges of learning.

Achievements are the treasure one finds out on one's adventures. And in the ancient tales, these shiny treasures are always really symbolic of transformation. The hero is transformed on the inside, and the whole world around the hero is also changed. Adventuring is a social business, achievements improve society, and inspire the next generation of heroes.

Achievements are the residues of the adventures and experiences that you have survived.

When you make a Bucket List, the approach is light and playful, it's useful to forget that you will bleed for every experience that you have.

After the adventure is done, and you find yourself in the tavern at the end of the world swapping stories with all the other adventurers. When you look back, it's safe to recall what you paid to earn the golden fleece that you have recovered from the great wild world.

The Fool in the Tarot is blissfully unaware of the suffering to come, which is precisely why the Fool has absolutely no fear of setting off on the next adventure. The Fool is no fool.

But the scar is the medal. And what is learning but a very specific set of scars, carved into our new neural pathways?

There is only one true superpower on this earth – sustained focus over time.

But what to focus on? The big secret is, it doesn't really matter.

We train young people to believe that everyone is born with a secret purpose hidden inside of them. What a profoundly useless idea! How many wasted years are spent on trying to discover what it is?

Pick anything. Double down.

There is nothing more toxic and seductive than the space of infinite possibility. If you don't move, you never have to close all the doors that going through one door will force you to close. And you'll remain paralysed, sat pondering for eternity which door to go through.

Get really good at something. And through that process, the world doesn't really narrow, it opens up in ways that are impossible to explain.

Get really good at learning, and you'll never, ever be bored.

"Is there any greater joy
than a hard fought for
and hard won achievement?

You can keep your spa
weekend, I won't choose
the easy road.

Delayed gratification
is the only gratification
for me!"

DO GREAT THINGS

It takes what it takes.

Set a goal so ambitious that even your failure will be spectacular. Some things take tenacity. You cannot fail if you do not stop. Some things take guts. Beyond the horizon of that fear is a new understanding waiting for you.

Some of these things just require you to remember the basics. Notice the greatness already present. Remember how much you used to enjoy simple pleasures, before life got so crazy.

Bucket Done it

Find a job I love

Find a way to love the job I currently have

Conquer a fear

Take a digital detox and unplug from the internet for a week

Tell someone my true feelings

Start a rainy day fund

Write a haiku

Make a heartfelt donation to a worthy charity

Bucket   Done it

○ ○   Learn to say no without feelings of guilt

○ ○   Start a gratitude journal

○ ○   Support a startup project on Kickstarter

○ ○   Create a time capsule and bury it

○ ○   Support a fundraising campaign on GoFundMe

○ ○   Master a new skills (change a car tyre, learn first aid, learn self defence etc.)

○ ○   Take a 24 hour vow of silence

○ ○   Volunteer

○ ○   Write a fiction story

○ ○   Write a poem

○ ○   Stay off Facebook for a week

○ ○   Let go of one painful memory

○ ○   Tell someone I love them

Bucket *Done it*

◯ ◯ Research and document my family tree

◯ ◯ Detox from social media for 48 hours

◯ ◯ Be honest about everything for a week

◯ ◯ Sign up to become a blood donor

◯ ◯ Sign up to be a bone marrow donor

◯ ◯ Sign up to be an organ donor

◯ ◯ Quit a bad habit

◯ ◯ Forgive someone

◯ ◯ De-clutter my life

◯ ◯ Plant a herb garden

◯ ◯ Make a list of 10 things that make me happy

◯ ◯ Cut out one toxic thing from my life

◯ ◯ Grow my own vegetables

◯ ◯ Commit to take the stairs and not the lift

Bucket Done it

○ ○ Make and sell something made by my own hand

○ ○ Write a gratitude list of all the things
I'm grateful for

○ ○ Draw someone's portrait

○ ○ Make a list of 3 books that I've always wanted to
read (and then read them)

○ ○ Teach somebody something: How to ride a
bike/learn to swim/how to cook a meal

○ ○ Visit a cemetery and place a bunch of flowers on a
neglected grave

○ ○ Draw a self-portrait

○ ○ Make a sculpture in clay

○ ○ Make a commitment to drink more water

○ ○ Write a short story

○ ○ Write a novel

○ ○ Write a song

Bucket *Done it*

○ ○ Send a handwritten letter to someone who lives very far away

○ ○ Write a letter to my future self, only to be opened in 10 years time

○ ○ Learn to cook a signature three course meal

○ ○ Read a book a month for a year

○ ○ Listen to a new podcast every week for a month

○ ○ Read a book that I started but never finished

○ ○ Call someone that I haven't spoken to in over a year

○ ○ Join a club or a team

○ ○ Volunteer at an archaeological dig

○ ○ Look up and reach out to an old school friend

○ ○ Live, study or work abroad

○ ○ Give myself permission to fail

Bucket

Done it

○ ○ Get re-Tweeted by a celebrity

○ ○ Clear my email inbox

○ ○ Mend something that's broken

○ ○ Adopt a rescue animal from a shelter

○ ○ Act in a play

○ ○ Reach out to someone who was inspirational to me and tell them how much they helped

○ ○ Go metal detecting

○ ○ Get picked up at the airport by someone holding a sign with my name on it

○ ○ Apologise to someone I hurt in the past

○ ○ Accept that life is not always fair

○ ○ Surprise a friend with a touch of kindness

○ ○ Plant a tree and watch it grow

○ ○ Take responsibility for the things in my life that I can change

"
*learn to love
the curve*
"

When you spend a lot of time learning new things,
and you should always be spending time
learning new things because:

"Once you stop learning you start dying."
Albert Einstein

So when you are going through the learning curve in many
different ways, learning skills and knowledge of different
kinds, you start to get really familiar with the learning
curve itself, and you start to recognise moments within it.
This is especially powerful because the way you
experience the learning curve will be unique to you. You'll
know your own demons better than anyone.

Even so, broad features of the curve are universal. It's
beginning is remarkably uniform...

When you start learning something new, there is always a rush of enthusiasm, a honeymoon. And it is always followed by a slough of despondence, a brick wall, a moment of crushing doubt. And you can stop there, most people do. The brain is excellent at coming up with compelling arguments for not wasting precious energy.

Or you can shuffle on, feeling a bit despondent, there is a phase of kind of stumbling through the dark that can feel utterly pointless, the bit of the project where you know for a fact you won't use the work you're doing because it's rubbish, the time you spend unravelling twenty hours of knitting because your tension is off.
But you keep doing it anyway.

Breakthrough.

Then it gives, you have sacrificed the lamb of your labour to the gods of learning and they have seen fit to grant you mercy. There is a moment of buzzing in the brain, you can almost feel the new synaptic connections being drawn. Ideas come. Flow comes. Real, measurable progress. I'm doing it mom! look no hands!

That is not the end of the learning curve. Learning is tough. It'll throw you again and again. And sometimes you need to just leave it for a bit. Also fine.

But if you know the learning roller coaster well, you'll be that bit less likely to fall off it.

And you'll discover that learning is the closest thing on earth to real magic.

Bucket *Done it*

○ ○ Throw a surprise party for someone close to me

○ ○ Write a list of 3 things that I have been putting off and then go out and do them

○ ○ Commit to slowing down

○ ○ Get followed on Social Media by a celebrity

○ ○ Conquer a fear

○ ○ Stand up and speak up for my beliefs

○ ○ Join a gym

○ ○ Go back to school

○ ○ Arrange a family reunion

○ ○ Complete the interactive book **Burn After Writing by Sharon Jones**

○ ○ Get my affairs in order

○ ○ Be part of my community - join a local work group

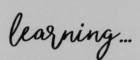

anything, makes you better at learning everything.

learning...

one thing, makes everything more interesting.

always end with learning, learning always
ends up an adventure.

learning...

something new makes you feel new.

Bucket | Done it

○ ○ Write a letter to the editor

○ ○ See a shooting star

○ ○ Start a 365 photo a day challenge

○ ○ Reach out and connect with a friend that I've lost touch with

○ ○ Do something new every month for a year

○ ○ Be an extra in a movie

○ ○ Compile the soundtrack of my life

○ ○ Abstain from alcohol for a month

○ ○ Have a games night with family or friends

○ ○ Look up and reach out to an old work colleague

○ ○ Start a fire without matches

○ ○ Give my car a name

○ ○ Cut out caffeine for a month

Bucket *Done it*

○ ○ Sponsor a child

○ ○ Start a journal

○ ○ Start studying something just for fun

○ ○ Have a school reunion

○ ○ Let go of one painful thought that I've been carrying

○ ○ Take a vow of silence for 24 hours

○ ○ Plant a seed and nurture it to grow

○ ○ Commit to questioning my convictions

○ ○ Take a photo of myself, once a month, every month, for the next 10 years

○ ○ Create my own recipe book

○ ○ Return to my childhood home and walk my old neighbourhood

○ ○ Create a side hustle

○ ○ Adopt/foster a pet

○ ○ Commit to taking the one risk in life that I would take if I knew I would not fail

○ ○ Create a family tradition

○ ○ Sign a petition for a cause that I really believe in

○ ○ Commit to choosing ethical and local shopping

○ ○ Say yes to everything for a day

○ ○ Grow a bonsai tree

○ ○ Commit to setting my alarm 30 mins earlier every day for a year (and gain 182 hours!)

○ ○ Sing in a choir

○ ○ Commit to picking up the street rubbish in my neighbourhood one day a week

○ ○ Go for a health check

○ ○ Try and inspire someone in some small way

Bucket *Done it*

○ ○   Make a will

○ ○   Write my autobiography using the interactive book **This Is My Life Story by Patrick Potter**

○ ○   Reach out and make contact with all of my neighbours that I don't know

○ ○   Repair something that's broken

○ ○   Look up and reach out to my childhood best friend

○ ○   Leave an eye-wateringly large tip for exceptional service

○ ○   Apologise to someone I have hurt deeply

○ ○   Develop a passive income stream

○ ○   Talk to my parents about their life before I was born

○ ○   Go a day without spending any money

○ ○   Plan to do something that scares me

"*personal development*"

You are your own work of art. Where do you want to put that light and shade?

Throughout your career, it's usually a good idea to play to your strengths. Personal development is more a game of facing up to your weaknesses.

What kinds of achievements could you aim for that address your inner demons? Because often the most gratifying achievements in life are the ones that nobody thinks you're capable of.

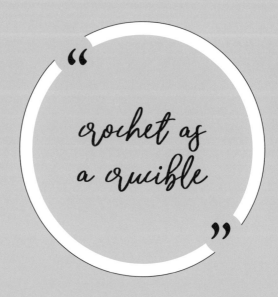

"crochet as
a crucible"

I once taught a crochet workshop.

High drama is all good, but sometimes it's the small adventures that unlock the big revolutions. Trying to learn to crochet might seem trivial. Nothing is trivial.

It's amazing how much emotional pain is buried in there under those failed attempts in childhood, the connection of the thing to a wider network of emotional memory, the parent you felt you disappointed, the sense of impotence when a sibling could do something you couldn't.

Great big capable adults with a litany of achievements behind them can crumble at the crochet hook, all of their demons coming to the fore, discovering an oblique way to foreground an internal conflict that you didn't even know was there.

Many of us have similar scars, especially around drawing, singing and dancing. Book a lesson doing something that scares you, something that really shouldn't scare you. Plan to do something so small and silly that you can't even believe how nervous it makes you to have a go. Experience feeling like you want to cry when your drawing / dance move / song turns out wrong.

Courage isn't always about bungee jumping.

Now relax and pick that crochet hook back up. Literally the only way you can fail is to stop trying. Every learning curve surrenders to the almighty force of our adaptive capacity.

Everything surrenders to sustained focus over time.

"
Nothing beats
kung fu.
"

START WITH A LIST
AND GET STUFF DONE

It started with a list...Some people take this stuff really seriously. Some people still be writing lists on the back of till receipts piled up and soggy on the kitchen counter.

Writing externalises obligations. It is a form of public commitment. Even more so if you share the list. Writing is the first step towards making an idea a reality. Even if that is only 'more bin bags'. Writing helps half an idea become a whole one.

Make a list of the changes that I want to make in my life

Make a list of **5** things that I have always wanted to do but have never done

1

2

3

4

5

Make a list of **5** things I need in my life right now

1

2

3

4

5

Make a list of the people that I need to forgive

Make a list of the people that I need to make more time for

A list of challenges to set myself for the next 12 months

GOALS

We've all had the SMART talk. We all know that goals are SPECIFIC, MEASURABLE, ACCURATE, RELEVANT and TIME BOUND. But we tend to allow our goals to become vague anxieties and unspecified phantoms stitched out of guilt. How do we beat that?

Pick one. Make it attainable. Make yourself accountable. Know yourself.

Sounds easy? Yeah right.

A goal is a simple thing to understand, but a hard thing to get right. Many people are having success with coaching for specific goals. Coaching seems to work very well for goals. In fact, the science of goal setting and achievement has had a huge amount of work poured in during the last few decades, mainly because it is profitable.

Goals are often super universal. Everyone wants to be fitter, happier, healthier and more productive. So double down on making your goal specific to you. What is your definition of fitter? What's your six week goal? What's your six month goal?

"

relationships

"

Relationship goals. We often take relationships for granted, but we need to make room for them on our bucket list too. What can we achieve in our relationships? We can target shared experiences, repair old injuries, have conversations we have been putting off. We can build new relationships, we can prioritise helping other people achieve the things on their bucket lists. Ultimately the only thing that gives us a sense of meaning is social life.

What is the point of having a bucket list if you have nobody to tell when you tick something off?

TWO'S COMPANY

#couplegoals

A bucket list doesn't have to be a solitary affair. Experiences are usually better with company. And nothing brings people together better than a shared experience. Remember back before your entire relationship was conducted in front of Netflix? Remember back before you became joint CEOs of the family affairs?

Yeah it was tiring wasn't it. But perhaps there's a few more adventures left yet...

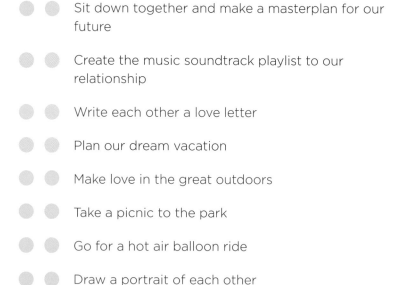

Bucket   Done it

○ ○ Sit down together and make a masterplan for our future

○ ○ Create the music soundtrack playlist to our relationship

○ ○ Write each other a love letter

○ ○ Plan our dream vacation

○ ○ Make love in the great outdoors

○ ○ Take a picnic to the park

○ ○ Go for a hot air balloon ride

○ ○ Draw a portrait of each other

○ ○ Complete a jigsaw together

Bucket   Done it

Go hiking together

Watch the sunrise and the sunset in a single day

Play a game of 20 questions

Go wild swimming

Learn salsa dancing together

Try a new hobby together

Go for a wine tasting experience

Cook dinner together

Create a mystery tour for one another

Recreate our first date

Take an exercise class together

Go on a road trip

Have a day at the horse races

Discover naturism together

Visit each others' hometowns

Go to a fancy dress party together

Bucket Done it

Stay in bed for 24 hours together

Train to take part in a fun run

Learn to tango

Make a scrapbook of memories

Take a pottery class together

Give each other a massage

Commit to a date night once a month for a year

Go glamping

Go for a bike ride together

Build a campfire and toast S'mores

Climb to the top of a mountain together

Host a couples games night

Draw caricatures of each other

Go camping together

Have a spa experience

Play a board game together

Bucket Done it

○ ○ Go to the theatre together

○ ○ Learn something new together

○ ○ Have fun with a game of truth or dare

○ ○ Break out of an escape room together

○ ○ Go cliff jumping together

○ ○ Adopt a shelter pet

○ ○ Plan a surprise trip for my partner

○ ○ Go to a masquerade ball

○ ○ Volunteer together in our local community

○ ○ Go on a road trip with no destination in mind

○ ○ Go watch a movie at a drive in

○ ○ Post each other a handwritten love letter

○ ○ Sign up for and complete an obstacle race

○ ○ Get matching tattoos

○ ○ Create a Christmas tradition together

○ ○ Binge watch an entire box set in a single weekend

Bucket   Done it

Take an RV trip across a country

Go tech free together for 24 hours

Tell each other a secret

Go back to our honeymoon destination

Take a workout class together

Have a couple's massage

Spend a night stargazing and trying to spot the planets

Throw a dart at a map and go wherever it lands

Sing a karaoke duet

Create a monogram using our initials

Take a helicopter ride together

Sponsor a child

Create a jar of ideas for date night

Take turns in saying 'yes' to everything for a day

Attend a film premier

Stay in a cabin in the woods

Bucket *Done it*

○ ○ Spend a night in a castle

○ ○ Create our relationship time capsule

○ ○ Go dog sledding

○ ○ Take part in a fun run together

○ ○ Plan a trip to somewhere we've never been

○ ○ Go backpacking

○ ○ Go skinny dipping

○ ○ Create a memory book together

○ ○ Start a side business together

○ ○ Foster a child

○ ○ Renew our wedding vows

○ ○ Go whitewater rafting

○ ○ Create our own coat of arms

○ ○ Cook an epic five course meal together

○ ○ Book a romantic trip in a classy hotel

○ ○ Throw a dart at a map and go somewhere spontaneous

ROMANTIC PLACES FOR COUPLES

When it comes to lovin' the setting is everything. What better way to write your love story than to literally **change the scene?** There's a reason that a cliché becomes a cliché. Take a lover to Paris. Heck, take 'em out for a moonlit stroll somewhere you can still see the stars. Take your romance to the most romantic places on Earth. Maybe you won't be the first but for a moment you'll be the only people on earth.

Bucket　*Done it*

- ◯ ◯　Take a gondola ride through the canals in Venice, Italy

- ◯ ◯　Climb to the top of the Eiffel Tower in Paris, France

- ◯ ◯　Take a romantic stroll on the beach in Maui, Hawaii, USA

- ◯ ◯　Watch the sun set in The Greek Islands, Oia, Santorini, Greece

- ◯ ◯　Wake up together in an overwater bungalow in The Maldives

- ◯ ◯　Take a romantic stroll on the beach in the Seychelles

- ◯ ◯　Watch giraffes and elephants from the comfort of a private terrace in a tented camp in Ruaha National Park, Tanzania

- ◯ ◯　Get married at the Little Church of the West in Las Vegas, Nevada, USA

Bucket *Done it*

○ ○ Take a drive along the Amalfi Coast and check out Positano before taking a ferry to Capri, Campania, Italy

○ ○ Explore the lush rainforests of Bali, Indonesia

○ ○ Go walking together in breathtaking scenery in The Lake District, Cumbria, England

○ ○ Have a winter wonderland experience husky sledding in Lapland, Finland

○ ○ Take a carriage ride through Central Park, New York, USA

○ ○ Spend a night watching the Northern Lights before retiring to the ice hotel in Lapland at Jukkasjarvi, Sweden

○ ○ Swim in crystal clear waters in Tahiti, French Polynesia

○ ○ Eat key lime pie and watch the sun set in Key West, Florida, USA

○ ○ Dine onboard the Venice Simplon Orient Express

○ ○ Go back to the place where we first met

○ ○ Walk hand in hand through Jardin Majorelle - Yves Saint Laurent in Marrakech, Morocco

"

big plans

"

What if we opened our own school?

What if we changed the way an entire industry worked?

What if we built some kind of incredible eco-farm where people from all over the world could come and learn about sustainable food production?

These are the kinds of plans that are so BIG they require an actual bona fide project manager.

Hey, why not? If it has been done then you can do it too.

EVERY DAY IS A SCHOOL DAY

The internet is the greatest tool for learning in history, and we use it for amusing cat videos. Teach yourself something. Anything. It's all out there. You can achieve more in ten hours of focus than you might imagine. Always. be. learnin'.

Bucket
Done it

- Learn to fly a plane

- Learn to drive

- Learn to change a car tyre

- Learn first aid

- Learn to play a musical instrument

- Learn to type

- Learn to knit/crochet/embroider

- Learn to play chess

- Learn to juggle

- Learn to sail

- Learn to speak a foreign language

- Learn how to say hello in sign language

Bucket *Done it*

◯ ◯ Learn a poem off by heart

◯ ◯ Learn to bake a cake

◯ ◯ Learn to read music

◯ ◯ Learn one new word a day for a year
(and use each one)

◯ ◯ Learn to say hello in 5 languages

◯ ◯ Learn to play a song on an instrument

◯ ◯ Learn to scuba dive

◯ ◯ Learn to dance

◯ ◯ Learn to waterski

◯ ◯ Learn yoga

◯ ◯ Learn to meditate

◯ ◯ Learn to code

◯ ◯ Learn how to draw

◯ ◯ Learn how to jump start a car battery

Bucket Done it

○ ○   Learn to sew

○ ○   Learn to perform the Heimlich Maneuver

○ ○   Learn to swim

○ ○   Learn how to improve my posture

○ ○   Learn skills how to de-stress

○ ○   Learn a card trick

○ ○   Learn how to cook a signature dish

○ ○   Learn a new word a day for a month

○ ○   Learn calligraphy

○ ○   Learn how to do CPR

○ ○   Learn how to say 'thank you' in five different languages

○ ○   Learn to touch type

○ ○   Learn my family history

○ ○   Learn how to play poker

dreams

Dream job, dream house, dream car, dream life. What does all this mean to you? Dreaming is a great way to investigate our own desires. Let yourself drift through the gardens of your fantasies. It's the dreams that keep coming back to you, the ones you can't leave alone, those are the dreams you actually want to catch hold of.

And we are magic animals, we can make our visions into realities. Along the way, something is lost and something is found. But the dream is a great place to start, even though the reality is never ever what you dreamed it would be...

A LIST OF THE THINGS
THAT I WANT MOST OUT OF LIFE

How are you ever going to know what you want if you never ask yourself what you want? It's a surprisingly difficult question to answer. The trick is to just make stuff up. You're not committed to any of this, it's a brain shower. Fill these pages. Write fast. Do not self edit. the exercise might just surprise you. You can do this any time you feel lost. Consider it a return to first principles.

"challenges"

A challenge is basically a goal with a
sense of drama.

Challenges are exciting, public, and carry a high
risk of failure. Challenges make great PR. If you
want to get the whole world interested in what
you're trying to do, make it into a challenge.
Challenges invite other people to join in.
Challenges can go viral.

A challenge should make people sit up and go
'YOU'RE GONNA DO WHAT!?'

A challenge can take the form of a wager,
a bet or a dare.

The difference between saying 'I'm going to cut
down on sugar' to saying 'I'm doing the 100 DAY
ZERO SUGAR CHALLENGE' is all about
the drama.

The second one is more exciting, and therefore
more likely to keep you motivated. The suffering
is part of the fun. Live blogging the awful
experience of sugar withdrawal would make great
social media. Telling people how you've stopped
taking sugar in your tea is not the same thing.

So here's some ideas for CHALLENGES to get you
thinking of how best to torture yourself next.

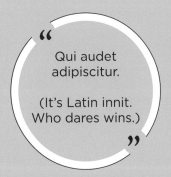

" Qui audet
adipiscitur.

(It's Latin innit.
Who dares wins.) "

GOAL SETTING

We all know the drill by now. 'It's gots to be specifical.' (Goal Setting Experts Say). When you look at your to-do list at six in the morning and it says GET HEALTHIER, well that's about as much use as a slap in the face with a kipper.

When it says EAT FIVE DIFFERENT COLOURS OF FRESH FOOD TODAY then at least you know where to start, and when to celebrate. So down that supergreens smoothie, put blueberries on your cereal and you're away to the races.

My health goal

My financial goal

My passion goal

My success goal

My learning goal

My change goal

My personal growth goal

My family goal

My relationship goal

My friendship goal

My giving back goal

My career goal

My creative goal

CHANGES TO MAKE

Time to make the change.

Let's try and summarise the billions of words of advice on this available on line. One at a time. Start so small you cannot fail. Tell everybody. Track your wins and try not to break the chain. Aim for 66 days to form a permanent habit. And remember the golden rule...most people need external pressure to meet commitments.

Pay someone to guilt trip you.
(The entire coaching industry explained.)

---

3 easy to make changes

1 _____

2 _____

3 _____

---

3 things I want to change but will take some effort

1 _____

2 _____

3 _____

3 things I want to change but will take a lot of effort

1

2

3

3 things I want to change but feel are impossible

1

2

3

The **1** thing that is holding me back from being the person I want to be

"pay it back
and pay it
forward"

We don't just want to watch the news anymore. We want to do something about it. We know that one day really quite soon, our children will be asking us very pointed questions about what we did when the climate crisis hit.

And the internet has made us hyper aware of how much worse life is for some people. We know that rampant inequality in our own countries has created the awful spectacle of child poverty in the richest countries in the world. We're not exactly uninformed, but we're often dazed and confused.

Overwhelmed.

How can we take some control of our own narrative?

How about setting some goals on the old Bucket List that allow us to meaningfully engage with these issues?

A lot of focus is placed on changes to everyday routines, and this is great but there are bigger, wider, deeper changes to be made before this all plays out.

Here's some ideas for achievements that pay back our debt to society and pay something forward to the world of the near future.

PAY IT BACK & PAY IT FORWARD

We are pack animals. Ever wonder why the richest countries in the world are the most depressed? Whoever dies with the most toys wins? Because the real 'The Secret' is we're happier when we're helping. If you're determined to believe we are selfish animals then remember, helping makes you look good. Doing good things for the tribe is the best way to get famous.

- Support animal rights
- Champion climate change
- Civil rights advocacy
- Stand up for racial inequality
- Champion universal healthcare
- Local initiatives and issues
- Campaign against gun violence
- Supporting refugees
- Food poverty
- Gender equality/LGBTQ advocacy
- Commit to fighting poverty

Bucket Done it

Social justice

Hate crime

Criminal Justice Initiatives

AIDS

Gender inequality

Social inequality

Veteran support

Help the homeless

Wildlife and nature initiatives

Domestic violence

Racism, racial inequality and prejudice

Censorship campaigning

Human rights advocacy

Boycott something

FILMS I NEED TO WATCH

Here's looking at you, kid. There's a reason some films are still quoted 80 years after they premiered. Some things go beyond successful to become the eternal lode stones of an entire culture. Doesn't matter if you watch them or not, they're a part of your cultural landscape like children making lightsaber noises or the silhouette of a carving knife and a running shower.

Watch the whole list and you'll find yourself with a better grasp of 20th century history than you ever got at school.

Bucket Done it

⬤ ⬤ Vertigo

⬤ ⬤ Citizen Kane

⬤ ⬤ 12 Angry Men

⬤ ⬤ Schindler's List

⬤ ⬤ 2001: A Space Odyssey

⬤ ⬤ Apocalypse Now

⬤ ⬤ Three Colours: Red

⬤ ⬤ Monty Python and the Holy Grail

⬤ ⬤ The Wolf of Wall Street

⬤ ⬤ Pulp Fiction

Jurassic Park

No Country for Old Men

Good Will Hunting

The Elephant Man

Pan's Labyrinth

Raging Bull

Chinatown

Gone with the Wind

On the Waterfront

The Hobbit

Das Boot

The Shining

Rocky

Finding Nemo

Eternal Sunshine of the Spotless Mind

Bucket   Done it

⚪ ⚪   Lawrance of Arabia

⚪ ⚪   A Clockwork Orange

⚪ ⚪   The Sixth Sense

⚪ ⚪   Metropolis

⚪ ⚪   The Sting

⚪ ⚪   Scarface

⚪ ⚪   The Pianist

⚪ ⚪   Amelie

⚪ ⚪   Indiana Jones and the Last Crusade

⚪ ⚪   Singing in the Rain

⚪ ⚪   12 Years a Slave

⚪ ⚪   Sunset Boulevard

⚪ ⚪   The Godfather

⚪ ⚪   Cinema Paradiso

⚪ ⚪   Taxi Driver

Bucket   Done it

○ ○   Star Wars

○ ○   Trainspotting

○ ○   Fargo

○ ○   Psycho

○ ○   La Haine

○ ○   Life is Beautiful

○ ○   The Silence of the Lambs

○ ○   One Flew Over the Cuckoos Nest

○ ○   Some Like it Hot

○ ○   Toy Story

○ ○   Saving Private Ryan

○ ○   Inception

○ ○   Deliverance

○ ○   Charlie and the Chocolate Factory

○ ○   Grease

Bucket Done it

The Good, The Bad and the Ugly

The Deerhunter

The Seventh Seal

Blue Velvet

The Shawshank Redemption

Once Upon a Time in the West

Casablanca

Avatar

Titanic

There Will Be Blood

Bohemian Rhapsody

La La Land

Alien

The Breakfast Club

Donnie Darko

Bucket Done it

○ ○   Blade Runner

○ ○   Papillon

○ ○   To Kill A Mocking Bird

○ ○   Bicycle Thieves

○ ○   Rashomon

○ ○   Monty Python and the Holy Grail

○ ○   Annie Hall

○ ○   The Rocky Horror Picture Show

○ ○   Jaws

○ ○   The Exorcist

○ ○   La Dolce Vita

○ ○   Raiders Of The Lost Ark

○ ○   . . . And re-watch the film I loved as a child

life goals

What is your legacy?

What's the title of your biography?

What's the main storyline in the movie
of your life?

These are bucket list items that define your
whole life story.

These are the ones that will remind you who
you are whenever you get lost in the weeds.

THE MASTERPLAN

We hate making choices, because making choices closes doors. But the worst of all possible outcomes is withering and stagnating in a room full of open doors. Sooner or later you just have to pick one. A good trick is to pretend you are someone else. It's dead easy to write a master plan for someone else. It's always obvious what they should do with their talents and opportunities. Then when you've written it, sign it in blood. (Metaphorically). Voila. You've tricked yourself into becoming dynamic.

Bucket   Done it

○ ○   The dream I want to realise

○ ○   The goal I want to reach

○ ○   The person I want to meet

○ ○   The event I want to experience

○ ○   The place I want to live

○ ○   The change I want to make

WELLNESS

Do the things that make you feel better. Why is it so goddam hard? Self care isn't selfish, but the layers of puritanism run deep in our culture. The voices in the back of your head telling you to prioritise anything and everything else.

Book something. Do it now. Your guilt about missing an appointment will defeat your guilt about doing something for your physical and mental health. Make a public commitment. Get a wellness buddy. Make a deal with your partner, trade off self care tokens. Organise the peeps at work into a wellness club, get on the group discount apps.

○ ○ Have a reiki session

○ ○ Relax in a flotation tank

○ ○ Spend time with a life coach

○ ○ Relax with a deep tissue massage

○ ○ Start keeping a journal

○ ○ Unwind with an aromatherapy session

○ ○ Try a new sport

○ ○ Book a counselling/therapy session

○ ○ Go vegetarian for a week

○ ○ Try pilates

○ ○ Go vegan for a week

Bucket

Done it

Make a commitment to stretch 10 mins every morning for a month

Walk 10,000 steps every day for a week

Cut out processed foods from my diet for a month

Complete a couch to 5k running programme

Meditate for 10 minutes a day for a month

Try a reflexology treatment

Try an acupuncture treatment

Try Tai' Chi

Reach out to a nutritionist to create a diet plan

Run a 5k/10k/marathon

Go for a health check

Take part in a triathlon

Detox for a week

Try yoga

Plan a fitness challenge that will stretch me

Walk 30,000 steps in a single day

Eat five a day for a month

Do one hour of exercise per day
(only 4% of my day!)

BOOKS I NEED TO READ

There is no better antidote to digital overload. Audio books totally count. And the evidence shows that you get a stronger emotional response to the climax of a novel than the climax of any film or TV show. You know it's good for you. If you've never read a book since primary school, ease yourself in. Start with five minutes a day. It takes time to adjust to the pace of reading after hours of doom scrolling social feeds. But when you do adjust, you will fall in love with it. 100% guaranteed.

To Kill a Mockingbird by Harper Lee

Pride and Prejudice by Jane Austen

The Fault in Our Stars by John Green

One Hundred Years of Solitude by Gabriel Garcia Marquez

1984 by George Orwell

Great Expectations by Charles Dickens

The Secret History by Donna Tartt

Alice's Adventures in Wonderland by Lewis Carroll

Frankenstein by Mary Shelley

Moby Dick by Herman Melville

I Capture The Castle by Dodie Smith

Bucket

Done it

The Sellout by Paul Beatty

The Lord of the Rings by J. R. R. Tolkien

In Cold Blood by Truman Capote

The Catcher in the Rye by J. D. Salinger

Jane Eyre by Charlotte Bronte

The Great Gatsby by F. Scott Fitzgerald

Lord of the Flies by William Golding

Brave New World by Aldous Huxley

Charlie and the Chocolate Factory by Roald Dahl

The Lion, The Witch and the Wardrobe
by C. S. Lewis

Animal Farm by George Orwell

Gone Girl by Gillian Flynn

The Outsiders by S. E. Hinton

The Grapes of Wrath by John Steinbeck

Catch-22 by Joseph Heller

The Goldfinch by Donna Tartt

Gulliver's Travels by Jonathan Swift

Bucket

Done it

○ ○ **Ulysses** by James Joyce

○ ○ **The Time Machine** by H. G. Wells

○ ○ **Gone with the Wind** by Margaret Mitchell

○ ○ **Little Fires Everywhere** by Celeste Ng

○ ○ **Dracula** by Bram Stoker

○ ○ **One Flew over the Cuckoo's Nest** by Ken Kesey

○ ○ **War and Peace** by Leo Tolstoy

○ ○ **A Christmas Carol** by Charles Dickens

○ ○ **A Clockwork Orange** by Anthony Burgess

○ ○ **Women in Love** by D. H. Lawrence

○ ○ **On the Road** by Jack Kerouac

○ ○ **A Passage to India** by E. M. Forster

○ ○ **Wuthering Heights** by Emily Bronte

○ ○ **The Color Purple** by Alice Walker

○ ○ **Slaughterhouse Five** by Kurt Vennegut

○ ○ **The Handmaid's Tale** by Margaret Atwood

○ ○ **The Alchemist** by Paulo Coelho

Bucket

Done it

○ ○ **The Secret Garden** by Frances Hodgson Burnett

○ ○ **The Diary of a Young Girl** by Anne Frank

○ ○ **The Harry Potter Series** – J. K. Rowling

○ ○ **Birdsong** – Sebastian Faulks

○ ○ **The Time Traveller's Wife** – Audrey Niffenegger

○ ○ **The Hitchhiker's Guide to the Galaxy** – Douglas Adams

○ ○ **Of Mice and Men** – John Steinbeck

○ ○ **The Adventures of Sherlock Holmes** – Arthur Conan Doyle

○ ○ **Les Miserables** – Victor Hugo

○ ○ The book I want to read

○ ○ And . . . re-read the book I loved as a child

SAVE THE PLANET

Small efforts = Huge Impact

Commit to learning more about how climate change damages our planet

Take a break from consumerism and commit to buying less 'stuff'

Start recycling

Book staycations for the next 12 months

Sign a climate petition

Spend one day a month picking up litter in my neighbourhood

Plant a tree

Say no to plastic bags

Buy a bike and commit to cycling more and driving less

Commit to selling or donating items I don't need

Only buy sustainably sourced seafood

Go paperless

Donate to environmental causes

Stop eating at food outlets with non-recyclable packaging/cutlery

Only buy compostable rubbish bags

Commit to taking the stairs

Save energy and switch to long lasting LED lightbulbs

Switch to an electric car

Start carrying a reuseable water bottle to limit plastic consumption

Volunteer with an environmental group

Do a beach clean up once a month for a year

Bucket *Done it*

○ ○ Start biking/walking/carpooling/using public transport to get to work

○ ○ Avoid single use plastic items

○ ○ Stop using wet wipes

○ ○ Go solar

○ ○ Grow a house plant

○ ○ Stop using single use plastics and switch to recyclable glass

○ ○ Commit to turning off electrical items when I'm not using them

○ ○ Stop buying items in plastic packaging

○ ○ Check my car tyre pressures monthly to make sure my car is energy efficient

○ ○ Join a climate march

○ ○ Go dark for a day – Unplug

Start taking showers and stop having baths

Bucket   Done it

Switch to a renewable engergy tariff

Pledge support to an environmental non-profit

Switch to zero waste beauty products

Switch to organic food

Volunteer for cleanups in my community

Commit to walking instead of driving for one day a week

Switch to an ethical bank

Switch to locally sourced ingredients

Start 'meat free' Mondays

Practice sustainable fashion – Donate or upcycle my old clothes, commit to buying used items

Switch from domestic and short haul flights to travelling by train or coach or boat

Unplug all appliances, electronics and other devices when I'm not using them

THIS YEAR'S MASTERPLAN

Take as many of your 'one day maybe' ideas as possible and stuff them into your calendar for the next 12 months. We live in the age of the decline of the West. Carpe the mother loving Diem comrade. Before the plagues, floods and fires shut the whole game down. Make a year plan that you know will fail, but fail gloriously. When you aim for the stars and miss you can still land on the moon.

Bucket   *Done it*

◯ ◯   Experience something

◯ ◯   Ask someone

◯ ◯   Fix something

◯ ◯   Try something

◯ ◯   Buy something

◯ ◯   Help someone

◯ ◯   Go somewhere

> **People overestimate what they can do in one year and underestimate what they can do in five.**

Bucket / Done it

◯ ◯ Find someone

◯ ◯ Mend something

◯ ◯ Give something

◯ ◯ Question something

◯ ◯ Create something

◯ ◯ Accomplish something

◯ ◯ See something

◯ ◯ Learn something

In a world of limitless possibility, which of these achievements would you choose? Forget about reality. Choose from the suggestions on the previous pages and alter, combine, remix, and expand.

Fill these pages. Don't think. Just dream.

my growth
TASK
LIST

Go back through your dream list and choose one actionable first step for each item.

The dream does not become reality, on it's journey toward reality it becomes something else.

> **This is the first day of the rest of my life!**

If I knew that I only had one year to live, this is what I'd do . . .